I0816028

gather

savor

share

Beloved Staff Meals from the
Aiāna Kitchen / Raghav Chaudhary

gather savor share

Figure.1

PHOTOGRAPHY BY CHRISTIAN LALONDE FOREWORD BY VIKRAM VIJ

Recipes are chef tested.

25 26 27 28 29   5 4 3 2 1

Cataloguing data is available from Library and Archives Canada
ISBN 978-1-77327-273-3 (hbk.)

Design by Natalie Olsen
Photography by Christian Lalonde / Photoluxstudio.com
Prop styling by Irene Garavelli
Food styling by Raghav Chaudhary

Editing by Michelle Meade
Copy editing by Marnie Lamb
Proofreading by Breanne MacDonald
Indexing by Iva Cheung

Printed and bound in China by Shenzhen Reliance Printing Co., Ltd.

Figure 1 Publishing Inc.
Vancouver BC Canada
www.figure1publishing.com

Figure 1 Publishing is located in the traditional, unceded territory of the xʷməθkʷəy̓əm (Musqueam), Sḵwx̱wú7mesh (Squamish), and səlilwətaɬ (Tsleil-Waututh) peoples.

RECIPE NOTES
Unless stated otherwise:
Black pepper is freshly ground.
Butter is unsalted.
Citrus juices are fresh.
Eggs are large.
Milk is whole.
Sugar is granulated.
Vegetables are medium-sized.

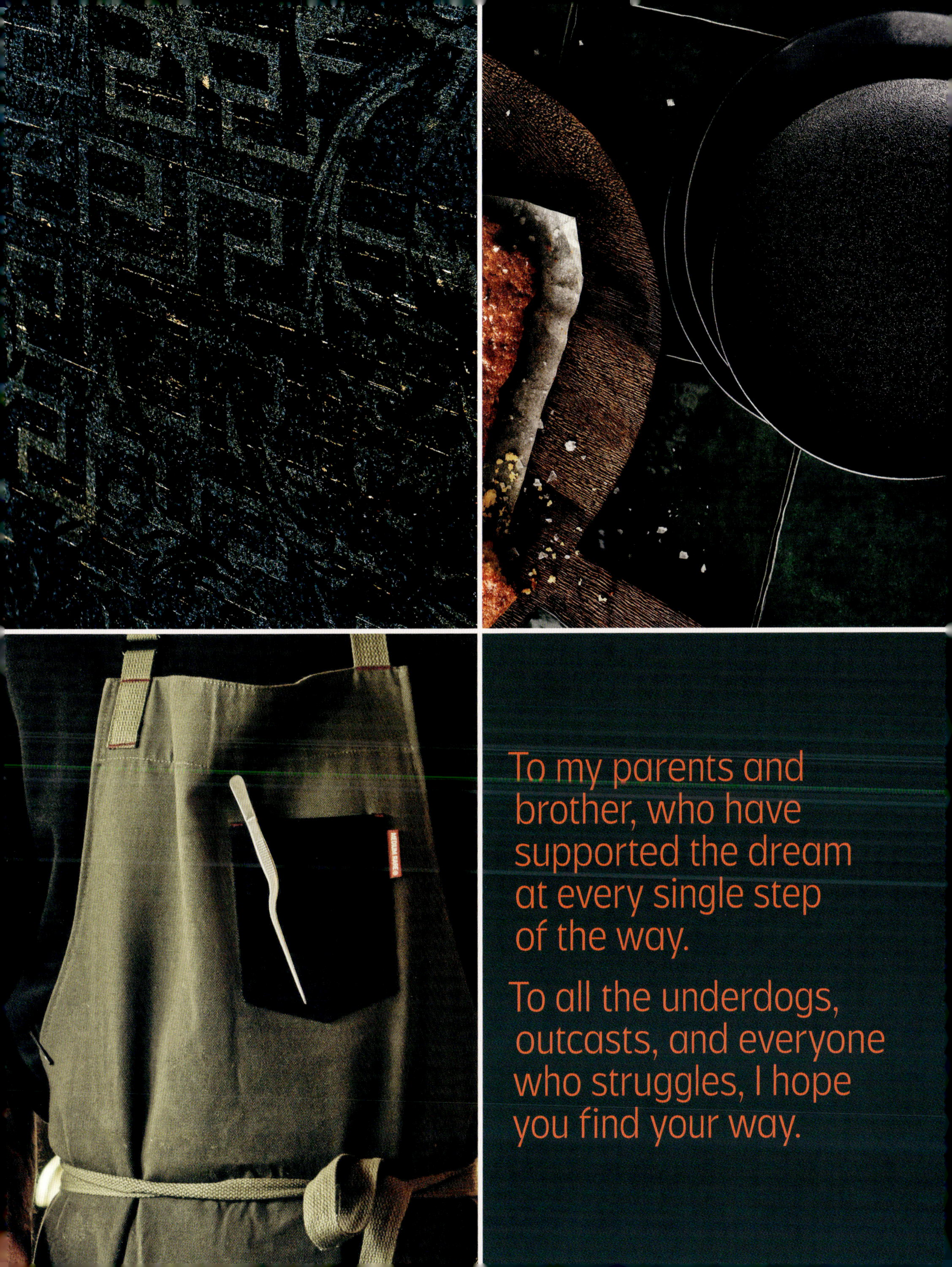

To my parents and brother, who have supported the dream at every single step of the way.

To all the underdogs, outcasts, and everyone who struggles, I hope you find your way.

contents

1/BREADS

2/GRAINS + LEGUMES

earth's
pantry

the garden's bounty

3/VEGETABLES

4/FISH + SEAFOOD

shoreside flavors

carnivore's corner

5/MEAT

6/DRINKS + DESSERTS

sips + sweet treats

7/THE BASICS

kitchen fundamentals

FOREWORD

I'll never forget when Anthony Bourdain famously came to my restaurant, Vij's, to shoot a segment for his TV show *No Reservations* in 2008. His preference was to visit the kitchen and dine with the team to get a better sense of the food and the people. You must know that my team in the kitchen were almost all women, and all of them from India. Very few, if any, spoke English, and Anthony didn't speak Punjabi. That evening, they communicated through food.

The people working for me had no idea who Anthony was, but like good hosts—and especially ones from India—they plied him with food. The dishes kept coming, and they seemed to get hotter one after the next. Anthony dutifully mopped up plate after plate until, with beads of sweat forming on his brow from an especially spicy lamb curry, he mouthed to me as if pleading for mercy: "I can't eat any more." I laughed at his predicament. "You need to tell them to stop," I said. "Or they'll feed you forever!"

More than my efforts to act as interpreter that night, it was food that brought us together. Worlds and traditions apart, around that table, we were one in the moment, savoring the flavors and essence of a good meal made from the heart and served with pride.

It is with this spirit in *Gather, Savor, Share* that chef Raghav Chaudhary invites us to embrace the comforting pleasures of a meal taken together—passing dishes, reaching for seconds, and even taking a cheeky swipe for the last piece of whatever was good that day. Preparing a meal for others is a supreme act of love, and breaking bread is among the most powerful and meaningful things we can do as humans. It builds understanding and respect, and dissolves differences to make equals of us all.

The food in these pages is truly Canadian. The recipes collected here celebrate the bounty of this great land and highlight with appreciation the diversity of those who call it home. With curiosity at its heart, *Gather, Savor, Share* is a beautiful testament to the power food has to connect us. From a quick Monday-night stir fry to a lavish weekend feast, each and every meal does more than fill our bellies—it nourishes our spirit and inspires our collective sense of belonging.

So, with this book as your guide, *gather* your folks, *savor* familiar and new flavors with curiosity, and *share* wholeheartedly in the experience only a good meal can create. Your world will become richer for it.

/ VIKRAM VIJ

Do something with passion or don't do it at all.

— CHRISTIAN BAU

PREFACE

Early mornings, late nights, and long, demanding days — working in a restaurant is known for its grueling hours and fast pace. That's why we cherish the rare moments when we can unwind, whether by swapping stories about the day's triumphs, laughing at our missteps, or simply sitting in silence to catch our breath. These chances to recharge don't come often, but there's one we can usually count on: the family meal.

Over the years, the staff meal, or family meal, has remained a constant in my life. It's a time to gather, share, and inspire each other. This cherished ritual unites the restaurant team, bringing together people from all walks of life — different creeds, cultures, and backgrounds — into one unforgettable moment. Here, we fuel each other, forge connections, and laugh (or lament) about the daily challenges of surviving this demanding industry.

The family meal has taught me that cooking is more than a necessity; it's a vibrant expression of creativity and connection. Food sustains us, but it can also be an act of generosity, a way to show love, and a means of sharing abundance. While food can unify, the motivations behind cooking vary. For chefs, it's an art form, a chance to shape and share our identity. For me, cooking is an immersive experience: art in motion, interactive and full of joy. This is the spirit I aim to capture in *Gather, Savor, Share* — a celebration of all that food is and everything it brings.

The family meal lies at the heart of my cooking style. It's about flavors and textures but also about people, stories, and origins. This cookbook reflects my core values and is filled with recipes I share with my family, whether at home or at work. My hope is that *Gather, Savor, Share* becomes more than just a cookbook. I want it to be stained, dog-eared, marked with notes and highlights, and eventually worn from use — just like the cookbooks I hold dear.

In the whirlwind of our fast-paced world, especially in the culinary industry, we often forget to slow down. But what if the kitchen could be your refuge? Take a moment to breathe, be present, and savor every experience — good or bad — because, trust me, it all serves a purpose. Cook with your heart. Let your emotions spill onto the plate, and see how food becomes your canvas.

I hope you find inspiration in these pages and share it with your loved ones — your "family," however you define it. Happy cooking.

/ RAGHAV CHAUDHARY

WHAT IS A FAMILY MEAL?

For those of us in the hospitality industry, we often find ourselves spending more time with our colleagues than with our own families. Enter the staff meal, or family meal: a shared breakfast, lunch, or dinner that brings the team together. It's more than just food; it's a moment for the restaurant crew to build stronger bonds and spark a sense of camaraderie and collaboration. Amid the chaos of the restaurant, the staff meal serves as a moment of connection and gratitude, a time when the tumult of service pauses to bring the team together.

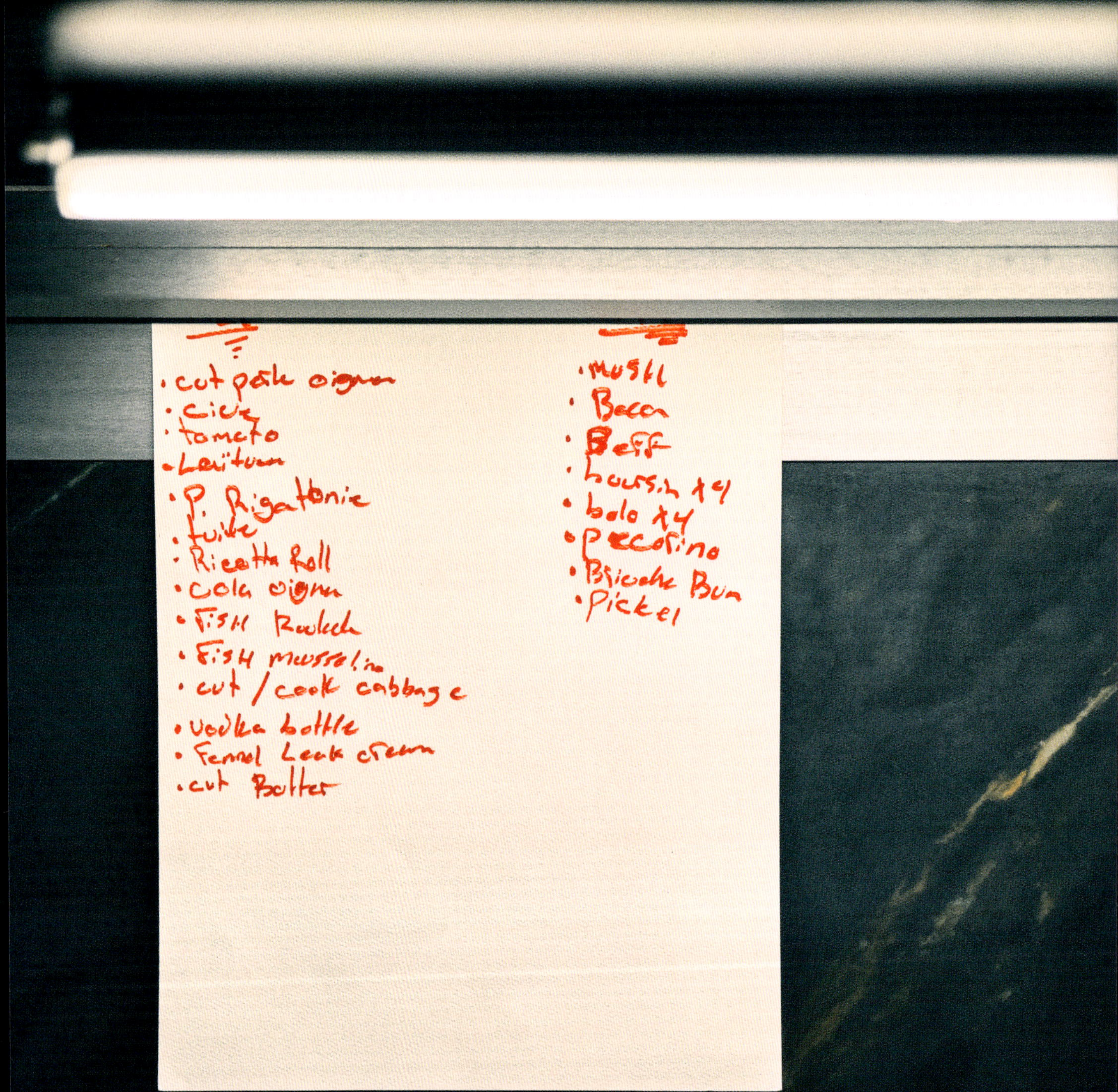

- cut pork oignon
- cive
- tomato
- Leitum
- P. Rigatonie
- fuike
- Ricotta Roll
- cola oignon
- Fish Roulade
- Fish mousseline
- cut / cook cabbage
- Vodka bottle
- Fennel Leek cream
- cut Butter

- Musli
- Bacon
- Beff
- boursin x4
- bolo x4
- pecorino
- Brioche Bun
- Pickel

Back in the day, I had the incredible opportunity to complete my externship through the Culinary Institute of America as a commis at the Michelin-starred restaurant COI in San Francisco, which was then led by the brilliant chef Matthew Kirkley. It was there that I was first introduced to the unforgettable experience of the family meal.

I often worked on salads and vegetable components for dinners, but my heart lay in the family meal. In nearly all the kitchens I've worked in, I've participated in preparing these meals, especially on my last day, turning them into a ritual of appreciation for my colleagues. These shared meals dissolved hierarchy, creating a space where chefs, line cooks, and dishwashers came together over food. It went something like this.

Every day at 3:45 PM, the family meal comprised a protein, a veg, a starch, and a salad. Saturdays, the only exception, were reserved for BLTs. We also had to work within the following parameters:

Use cost-effective ingredients.

Use trimmings.

Do not make anything soupy.

Prepare a drink if there is time or trim.

Make something sweet only for special occasions.

Prepare a family meal on your last day.

These are the ideal ground rules for a flawless family meal, and I bring them to life in Aiāna's kitchen. But ultimately, the real goal is simple: cook up enough to satisfy every hungry mouth around the table!

The family meal is often the only break we get during a shift, and it's usually a time of relaxation and camaraderie. I've witnessed these meals spark joy, recharge tired spirits, and even boost morale. But they can also have the opposite effect: unleashing chaos and triggering panic. Since you never know what kind of day someone is having or mood they're in, you can't always predict who might need the comfort that comes from sharing a meal. For me, the family meal is the perfect opportunity to connect with the diverse personalities that make up the restaurant team.

At a restaurant, preparing food for our colleagues, bosses, and friends comes with a sense of responsibility. It's more than just a meal; it's the fuel that powers us through the day. There's a fine line between abundance and restraint. The key is to keep the meal simple and satisfying. No need for over-the-top creations with exotic ingredients – just tasty, practical dishes that hit the spot. After all, the simplest things are often the best.
(Save the tweezers for service!)

Preparing a family meal is more than just cooking; it's a chance to communicate who you are as a chef and connect with those around you. Whether through your creativity, cultural roots, or personal culinary style, each dish tells a story. Cook what you love to eat, and bring flavors that spark memories. After all, the joy of sharing a meal is just as important as savoring the food itself. It's all about creating moments together.

Many of these principles can easily be adapted for home life. Take Aiāna, for example. Behind the scenes, the back-of-house team works fluidly to prepare dishes before or after a service, while the front-of-house crew quickly sets up the dining area, arranging the tables, cutlery, and flatware with precision. At home, a family of four can put this into practice: parents can prepare the meal, while young children pitch in by setting the table. On a larger scale, we live in an age where sustainability is key, and as consumers, we have a responsibility to care for the land, sea, and air. This mindset isn't just for restaurants. It's something we can all incorporate into our own kitchens, whether we're whipping up a quick weeknight dinner for roommates or sharing a late-night snack with friends.

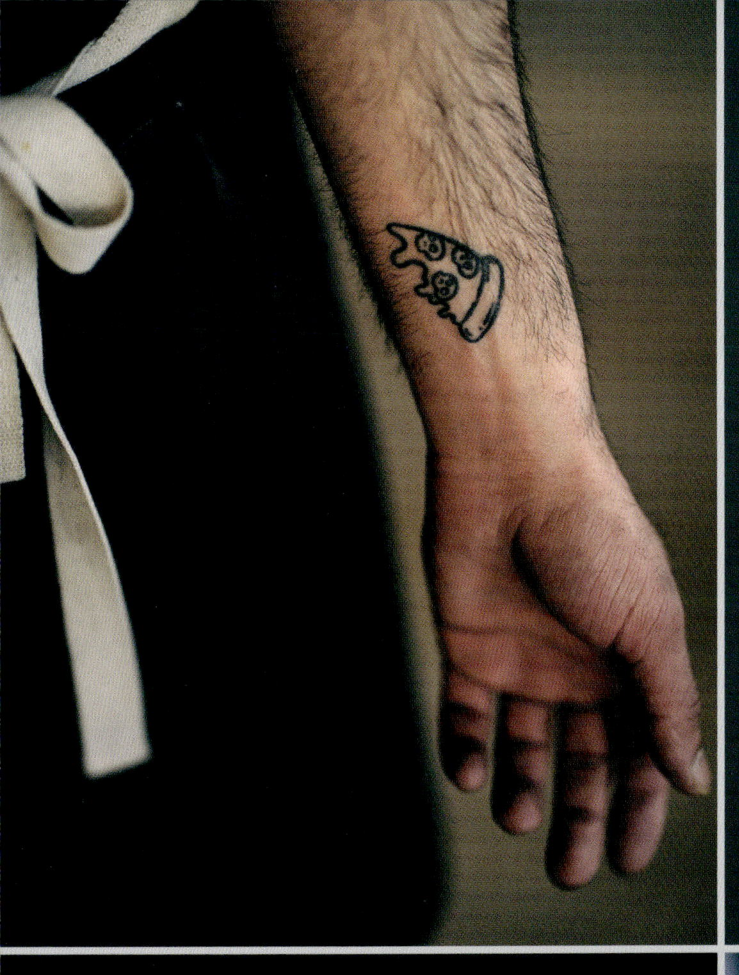

While the kitchen environment can feel demanding at times, it can be equally as rewarding — and these are the moments we savor. Cooking and the attention to detail can be revelatory, offering insight into the cook's world, identity, history, and, to an extent, their future. It is personal.

HOW TO USE THIS BOOK

Gather, Savor, Share is here to inspire you to become a better cook! Inside, you'll find a mix of my all-time favorite family dishes, like Mom's Spinach and Onion Pakoras / PAGE 93 and Daal Makhani / PAGE 72, alongside some lesser-known gems like Ricotta and Guanciale Rigatoni with Gremolata / PAGE 130. These unfamiliar recipes aren't just about delicious food – they're designed to stretch your skills and excite your taste buds (don't worry, they're just as mouthwatering as the familiar ones!). Some recipes, such as Garlic Pull-Apart Bread / PAGE 62 and Montreal-Spiced Steak / PAGE 135, dive into essential techniques and key ingredients that can make all the difference between a good dish and a great one. I'll be right there with you, guiding you through each step to make sure you nail it every time.

I truly believe that recipes aren't meant to be followed to a tee. They're not sacred text but rather starting points that invite you to make them your own. Think of them as blueprints with plenty of room for creativity. I encourage you to cook according to your tastes, your kitchen, and the people you're cooking for. The kitchen is the heart of the home, and cooking is the rhythm that keeps it alive.

Remember those little touches your mom or grandmother added to a dish, those special tweaks that made it unforgettable? That's the magic I strive for in my own family meals. Cooking from the heart is what makes every bite wholesome and delicious. So if something doesn't suit your taste, leave it out! If you want more heat, pile on the chilies! Don't be afraid to color outside the lines and make these recipes your own. Sure, it might feel a little clumsy at first – like learning any new skill – but with practice, trial, and error, you'll gain confidence.

Designed to be a valued resource, the cookbook is also peppered with useful advice, tips, and techniques to help you best express your cooking.

A daily routine in a restaurant kitchen is key to maintaining efficiency, consistency, and cleanliness. It ensures smooth operations, from prepping ingredients to plating dishes, which is especially critical during busy service times. Home cooks can benefit from a similar routine.

A DAY AT AIĀNA

8:00 AM

The AM team begins their shift, setting up the restaurant and organizing ingredients and tools for service. Lunch is just around the corner, so the clock is ticking.

9:00 AM

Deliveries of produce and supplies arrive, and it's crucial that the team inspects everything carefully to ensure quality. The goods must then be put away while cooks and serving staff prepare for service.

10:00 AM

This is when I arrive. I check in on the morning's progress and make sure we're on track for lunch. Depending on the day, a quick breakfast might be prepared for the team, giving us a moment to regroup before the first rush.

11:00 AM

Service begins. Orders start pouring in as the lunch rush takes off. Our downtown location means our guests typically have an hour for lunch, so service needs to be swift. You'll hear me shout, "Fire one black walnut, fire one grains, second-course scallops and salmon. Fire, fire, fire...!"

12:00 PM

By now, the kitchen management team — the chef, chef de cuisine, pastry chef, and sous chef — are in full swing. We execute lunch service and then start prepping for the family meal. One person is tasked with preparing a meal for the team. A mediocre family meal leads to low morale, so we ensure it's made with care and love.

1:00 PM

Lunch service winds down, and we shift focus to dinner prep. With just four hours to prepare, time is critical. Any issues must be addressed now.

2:00 PM

"Fifteen minutes early is on time." Everyone is ready to tackle the evening ahead. The pressure's on, the heat is high, and there's no room for mistakes.

3:00 PM

Customers trickle in for mid-afternoon snacks or drinks, often handled by the sous chef. The social hour rush comes and goes, and the day moves on.

TRIMS TO TRIUMPHS

What happens to all the left-over trimmings accumulated throughout the day? A team member can use them to create a snack. It's a great way to bond, spark creativity, and reduce food waste!

4:00 PM

The kitchen is filled with the aromas and chatter of the family meal. This moment is eagerly awaited, sometimes for days. Under the ticking clock, we scarf down our meal before diving back into the work. Saturdays are special: we're closed for lunch, and instead, we set up a long communal table. This day's family meal is a time to reflect on the week, celebrate birthdays, or bid farewell to a colleague. But, as always, once the meal is done, it's back to work.

HEAVY PLATES = DEAD WEIGHT

Make sure the family meal doesn't send everyone into a food-induced coma. A heavy meal is vital for restaurants, but trust me, a heavy dish at home will leave everyone lethargic and groggy. Keep your cooking light and nutritious; after all, it's your responsibility to keep the team alive!

5:00–9:00 PM

Dinner service begins. Everything is in place, and we're ready for the night. This is show-time — the culmination of all our efforts. Whether expediting a fine-dining dinner rush, hosting friends at home, or cooking for family, this is the moment we live for.

10:00 PM

"Kitchen, close" — no two words sound sweeter to a cook. We scrub away the day's work, reset, and prepare for tomorrow. This routine is a constant cycle that those of us in the restaurant world can't help but fall in love with.

SMART SPACE, SMARTER COOKING

Adapt your cooking to your space. The less space you use, the less you'll need to clean up. So make your space work smarter, not harder.

COOKING METHODS + TECHNIQUES

Mastering foundational cooking techniques is essential for cooks of all levels. These methods not only improve precision and efficiency but also unlock the full potential of flavors and textures. As skills grow, so does the ability to innovate, adapt recipes, and experiment with confidence.

BLANCHING involves briefly boiling vegetables (or other foods) and then quickly cooling them in ice water. This technique helps preserve nutrients and keeps vegetables crisp and vibrant, making it ideal for dishes that require freshness and color.

DE-GASSING refers to removing excess air or gas bubbles from a mixture, typically in baking or fermentation. For example, in bread-making, dough traps gases produced by yeast. De-gassing involves gently pressing or kneading the dough to release these bubbles, helping create a finer texture and ensuring even rising.

EMULSIFYING is the process of combining two liquids to form a stable mixture. A classic example is mayonnaise, which is a stable emulsion, unlike a vinaigrette, in which the liquids may form a looser bond. Stabilizers like mustard, egg yolk, or dried fruit can help strengthen the emulsion.

FERMENTATION is a natural process where microorganisms, such as yeast or bacteria, break down sugars and other compounds in food. This ancient preservation method produces gases, acids, and alcohols, which alter the flavor, texture, and nutritional value of the food. For instance, in bread-making, yeast ferments sugars in the dough to produce carbon dioxide, causing the dough to rise. In yogurt, bacteria ferments milk, giving it a tangy taste.

FOLDING is a gentle technique used to combine lighter ingredients, like whipped cream or beaten egg whites, with heavier mixtures without deflating them. The goal is to preserve the air bubbles, creating a fluffier, lighter texture.

THE MAILLARD REACTION occurs when proteins and sugars are cooked at high heat, resulting in browned food with rich flavors and aromas. When you sear steak, bake bread, or roast vegetables, the Maillard reaction enhances the food's taste and color, creating complex flavors and appealing scents.

MIREPOIX is a flavor base in French cuisine, made of two parts onion, one part carrot, and one part celery. Cooking these vegetables in fat releases their flavors, creating a delicious foundation for soups, stews, sauces, and more. It's a simple yet powerful way to add depth and richness to many dishes.

PICKLING is a preservation method where produce (or even proteins) is soaked in an acidic mixture of vinegar, sugar, salt, and spices. Pickling can be done either hot or cold. Cold pickling preserves the integrity and crunch of the food, while hot pickling softens it and develops a naturally sweeter flavor over time.

RESTING is the practice of letting hot foods sit after cooking to enhance flavor and texture. For meats like steak or chicken, resting for five to fifteen minutes helps redistribute juices, making meats juicier and more tender. Allowing baked goods such as bread or cookies to rest helps set their structure, making them easier to slice and less likely to fall apart.

SOUS VIDE is a cooking method where food is sealed in a plastic bag and cooked in a precise low-temperature water bath. This method ensures even cooking and helps retain moisture and flavor. It's commonly used for meats, vegetables, and even desserts. After sous vide cooking, food is often quickly seared for a nice finish and added texture. The table below provides a quick reference for crafting exceptional sous vide dishes. It outlines key elements – such as fat, aromatics, temperature, and time – optimized for various foods. This enables you to replicate professional-quality results with ease.

FAT	AROMATICS	TEMP	TIME	POST-SOUS VIDE COOKING METHOD
BONELESS PORK CHOP				
LARD	CINNAMON NUTMEG WHOLE CLOVES	**140°F**	**60** MINUTES	GRILLED
CHICKEN BREAST				
CHICKEN FAT	ORANGE CUMIN PAPRIKA	**150°F**	**60** MINUTES	GRILLED/SEARED/ROASTED
PAN-ROASTED SALMON FILLET				
BUTTER	LEMON THYME GARLIC	**125°F**	**30** MINUTES	TORCHED
NY STRIP LOIN				
TALLOW	MONTREAL STEAK SPICE ROSEMARY BAY LEAF	**128°F**	**45** MINUTES	GRILLED/SEARED/ROASTED
BUTTER-BASTED POTATOES				
BROWN BUTTER	BAY LEAF BLACK PEPPER SALT	**194°F**	**60** MINUTES	AIR-FRIED/CONVECTION-BAKED

KITCHEN ORGANIZATION

My mother always says that a cluttered environment equals a cluttered mind, and I agree with her 100 percent. When handling food, we have a duty to keep the ingredients freshly stored in a safe manner to prevent anyone from getting ill. The last thing you want is to turn what was intended to be a special moment into a moment your guests will regret. Therefore, it is vital to always maintain organization and cleanliness. Keep all surfaces sanitary, wash your hands constantly, do not cross contaminate, and wash as you go. Following proper food handling methods allows you to adapt more easily to any kitchen situation or guest request. Keep everything in its place, and put it back when you are done. Trust me, the last thing you want is to have to clean up an entire kitchen after spending all day cooking. At the restaurant, we deep clean the kitchens every Saturday. (Oddly, it has become therapeutic and [sort of] fun!)

I always set up a station for the task at hand. For example, I center myself behind a large wooden cutting board over a non-slip mat. I zone my ingredients: one for unprocessed ingredients and another for processed items. I set up a few towels, a sharp knife, a honing rod, a container for the required tools, and two other containers (one for usable trim and one for food waste).

CHAOS CONTROLLED *Repackage open items into containers, and label them with both the date they were opened and the expiry date. This helps maintain freshness and keeps your pantry organized.*

EVERYDAY FEASTS: MENUS FOR ALL OCCASIONS

This collection of vibrant, delicious menus is designed to inspire your next meal, offering a mix of flavors, textures, and colors to excite your taste buds and elevate everyday dining. But here's the fun part: these menus are just the starting point! Use them as a springboard for your own creativity. Swap ingredients, pair dishes differently, or add a personal twist. The possibilities are endless.

MY FAMILY'S TABLE

The Best Butter Chicken
PAGE 124

Mom's Spinach and Onion Pakoras
PAGE 93

Poppy and Nigella Seed Naan
PAGE 63

Daal Makhani
PAGE 72

Basmati Pilaf
PAGE 71

Mint Raita
PAGE 169

Chai Snickerdoodles
PAGE 151

Mango and Cardamom Lassi
PAGE 145

Bombay Gin Cocktail or Alexander Keith's IPA

COUNTRY COOKING

The Gunslinger's Turkey Chili
PAGE 126

New Potatoes with Paprika
PAGE 100

Smoked Gouda and Jalapeño Cornbread
PAGE 60

Carolina Gold Rice
PAGE 66

Ramp Ranch
PAGE 169

Chocolate Chip Cookies
PAGE 150

Bourbon Sour or Lager Beer

ASIAN NIGHT MARKET

Honeyed Walnut Shrimp
PAGE 118

Cucumber and Kimchi Salad
PAGE 81

Scotty's Fried Rice
PAGE 74

Chili-Garlic Oil
PAGE 176

Matcha and Red Bean Madeleines
PAGE 149

Original Soju or Tsingtao

OG ITALIAN

Ricotta and Guanciale Rigatoni with Gremolata
PAGE 130

Milk-Fried Cauliflower
PAGE 98

Garlic Pull-Apart Bread
PAGE 62

Stewed Tomatoes and Basil
PAGE 177

Parsley Aioli
PAGE 172

Negroni, Chianti, or Peroni

THAI FOOD

Pad Kra Pao
PAGE 132

Ginger-Peanut Papaya Salad
PAGE 82

Lemongrass and Coconut Jasmine Rice
PAGE 70

Sesame Kewpie
PAGE 171

Japanese-Style Fruit Sandwich
PAGE 156

Mai Thai, Moscow Mule, or Riesling

LISTEN UP *The best flavor combinations often come from support staff who may lack formal experience but bring a passion for food. Their ideas reflect the meals they enjoy at home and in their cultures. By listening, we can gain invaluable insights into food. In restaurants, cooks often use family meals to test flavors or explore new ideas. Try this at home: when friends or family cook for you, ask about the ingredients, traditions, and methods. Curiosity can lead to joyful culinary discoveries.*

TACO NIGHT

Fire-Roasted Lamb Birria Tacos
PAGE 140

Street-Style Elotes
PAGE 90

Pão de Queijo
PAGE 56

Arroz Rojo
PAGE 76

Cantina Guacamole (with Tortilla Chips)
PAGE 168

Dulce de Leche Churros
PAGE 153

Margarita or Modelo Especial

STEAK DINNER

Montreal-Spiced Steak
PAGE 135

Grilled Brassicas with Roasted Garlic-Lemon Vinaigrette
PAGE 99

Olive and Thyme Focaccia
PAGE 54

Shroom Risotto
PAGE 75

Chimichurri
PAGE 166

Vanilla Ice Cream
PAGE 158

Tempranillo Rojo or Guinness

MEDITERRANEAN

Falafels

PAGE 96

Fattoush

PAGE 86

Saffron Pita

PAGE 52

Steamed Quinoa

PAGE 66

Sumac Tzatziki

PAGE 167

Spicy Dill Pickles

PAGE 174

Pink Pickled Turnips

PAGE 174

Napa Valley Rosé or
Floral Cold Brew Tea

While pairings are not common in the setting of a family meal, Aiāna's wine and drinks list is a vital component of the restaurant. I've included optional drink pairings throughout to impart more flavor to the home dining experience. Pairings become an extension of the palate, mainly to bring out the best of the meal. Bear in mind, this does not have to be an alcoholic pairing; for instance, a hot chocolate with a dessert or an ice-cold lemonade with sprigs of fresh mint to complement the blazing heat of a curry will do. Be creative by exploring your palate further, and consider it an extension of the chef's intention and how you prefer the guest to taste the food.

Wine at the table is like an extra ingredient. It will add to the dining experience created by the family chef by complementing or contrasting the flavors and aromas coming from the plate. Grand wines are not essential for success; a simple wine can easily make a late-night sandwich into a meal worth taking the time to enjoy.

— ROBERT LEMIEUX

the recipes

breads

1

MAKES **12** / PREP: **15** MINUTES + **16** HOURS PROOFING AND CHILLING TIME / COOK TIME: **15** MINUTES

BANNOCK

A true North American classic, bannock is hearty, rustic, and packed with history. With Indigenous roots, it carries the essence of resilience and tradition, blending cultural heritage with the universal appeal of warm, homemade bread. It's the perfect companion to soups or stews or can be simply enjoyed with butter and jam.

INGREDIENTS

5⅓ cups all-purpose flour
2 tsp baking powder
1¼ tsp salt
1 Tbsp sugar
1 Tbsp honey
1½ tsp instant yeast
2 cups warm water
Canola oil, for deep-frying
Salt, to taste
Whipped Honey Butter (page 176) or Muddled Berries (page 175), to serve

In a stand mixer fitted with a hook attachment, sift together flour, baking powder, salt, and sugar.

In a small bowl, combine honey, yeast, and water. Slowly pour the liquid into the dry ingredients and mix for 6–8 minutes, scraping the sides of the bowl.

Transfer the dough to a large lightly greased bowl and set aside at room temperature for 4 hours. Refrigerate overnight.

Remove the dough from the fridge and ferment at room temperature for another 4 hours.

Preheat oven to 400°F. Line a baking sheet with parchment paper.

Pour oil into a deep fryer or deep saucepan and heat to a temperature of 350°F. Using your hands, pull the dough into irregular shapes roughly the size of a golf ball. Carefully lower the dough into the pan, taking care not to splash hot oil. Deep-fry for 4–6 minutes, until golden brown. Transfer to a paper towel–lined plate to drain. Season with salt, then transfer to the prepared baking sheet and bake for 8 minutes, until crisp and golden.

Serve hot with honey butter (or muddled berries).

SAFFRON PITA

This soft, pillowy pita is enhanced with delicate, aromatic saffron, which imparts a beautiful golden hue and a subtle fragrance. Perfect for dipping, stuffing, or tearing into as a side, this pita is the ideal vehicle for saucy curries and stews.

INGREDIENTS

3 cups bread flour (divided), plus extra for dusting
2¼ tsp instant yeast
1 tsp saffron
1¼ cups warm water
¼ cup Greek yogurt
2 Tbsp extra-virgin olive oil
1 tsp honey
1 tsp salt

In a large bowl, whisk ¾ cup of bread flour, yeast, and saffron. Pour in water. Set aside for 10 minutes, until bubbles begin to form.

Add the remaining 2¼ cups of flour and other ingredients and mix to form a wet dough.

Transfer the dough to a lightly floured surface and knead by hand until smooth and elastic. Place the dough in a large greased bowl, then cover and set aside for 1–2 hours, until doubled in size.

De-gas the dough by pressing it down gently with your fingertips. Cut the dough into 8 even pieces, then roll them into balls. Cover, then set aside to rest at room temperature for 30 minutes.

Preheat a baking sheet lined with parchment paper in the oven at 350°F.

Carefully place the dough balls on the hot sheet. Bake for 25 minutes, until puffed and golden.

COLD-FERMENTED PIZZA DOUGH

The secret to amazing pizza? It's all in the dough! This cold-fermented recipe builds up incredible flavor and texture the longer it rests. The result? A crust that's crispy, chewy, and perfectly airy — exactly how pizza should be. One bite, and you'll ditch store-bought for good! Cold fermentation, through the control of temperature and time, allows for the development of deeper flavor. The fermentation process is slowed down — often referred to as being "retarded" in baking — which contrasts with the faster fermentation at room temperature. This slower process gives the sugars more time to convert, resulting in a more complex and flavorful bread.

INGREDIENTS

3½ cups all-purpose flour, plus extra for dusting
1½ Tbsp extra-virgin olive oil
1 tsp sugar
½ tsp active dry yeast
1¼ cups water
1¾ tsp salt
Tomato sauce
Pizza toppings

PAIRING Oatmeal Stout

In a stand mixer fitted with a hook attachment, combine flour, oil, sugar, and yeast. Pour in water and mix on low speed until a loose dough is formed. Add salt and mix on medium speed for 10–12 minutes.

Place the dough in a large container, cover, and refrigerate to proof overnight.

Preheat oven to 475°F.

Place the dough on a work surface lightly dusted with flour. Using a bench scraper, divide the dough in half and form into balls. Using your hands, stretch out each ball of dough to fit the shape of a pizza pan. The dough doesn't have to be perfect — it's rustic!

Add tomato sauce and your favorite toppings. Bake for 12 minutes for a crispy, well-done pizza. Charring is acceptable!

RIND OVER MATTER *Keep all small ends of cheese in a container in the freezer. They can add flavor to recipes like Pão de Queijo (page 56) and mac 'n' cheese or serve as emergency pizza toppings! Hard cheese rinds, such as Parmesan, can be wrapped in a cheesecloth (to preserve flavor and minimize waste) and added to tomato sauces or soups.*

MAKES **1** LOAF / PREP: **15** MINUTES + AT LEAST **10** HOURS RESTING AND PROOFING TIME / COOK TIME: **30–35** MINUTES

OLIVE AND THYME FOCACCIA

This focaccia is a Mediterranean dream! The combination of briny olives and fragrant thyme transforms a simple loaf into a flavorful masterpiece. It's perfect for snacking, serving as a side, or stealing the spotlight on a charcuterie board.

STARTER

1⅓ cups all-purpose flour
1 tsp instant yeast
½ cup water at 167°F

FOCACCIA

4½ cups all-purpose flour
1½ cups Starter (see here)
1½ tsp instant yeast
¼ cup extra-virgin olive oil, plus extra for drizzling
1¾ cups water
2 tsp flaky sea salt, plus extra to taste
3 Tbsp chopped Calabrese olives
2 Tbsp chopped sun-dried tomatoes
2 tsp thyme leaves
2 tsp rosemary
1 tsp black pepper

STARTER In a small bowl, combine all ingredients and knead lightly. Transfer to a small container and set aside at room temperature overnight.

FOCACCIA In a stand mixer fitted with a hook attachment, combine flour, starter, yeast, and oil. Add water and mix on low speed. Add salt and mix for 5 minutes on medium speed, until the dough is smooth and elastic.

Transfer the dough to a large well-oiled bowl. Cover and set aside to proof at room temperature for 45 minutes–1 hour, until doubled in size.

Oil your hands, then fold the dough over itself 3 times, taking care not to deflate it completely.

In a small bowl, combine olives, sun-dried tomatoes, thyme, and rosemary. Add three-quarters of the olive mixture to the dough and fold again.

Transfer the dough to a greased baking pan, then set aside to proof for 1 hour, until doubled in size.

Preheat oven to 375°F.

Oil your hands again, then use your fingertips to press the dough down. Top the dough with the remaining olive mixture, season with salt and pepper, and drizzle with oil. Bake for 30–35 minutes, until golden brown.

MAKES **8** ROLLS / PREP: **15** MINUTES / COOK TIME: **20** MINUTES

PÃO DE QUEIJO

These chewy and completely addictive Brazilian cheese breads are made with tapioca flour and have a one-of-a-kind texture — crispy on the outside, soft on the inside. Perfect for a snack, appetizer, or party treat!

INGREDIENTS
⅓ cup canola oil, plus extra for greasing
⅔ cup milk
1 egg
1⅓ cups tapioca flour
½ tsp salt
⅓ cup grated mozzarella, frozen
⅓ cup grated Parmesan, frozen
⅓ cup grated cheddar, frozen

PAIRING Cachaça

Preheat oven to 375°F. Line a baking sheet with parchment paper, then grease.

In a small bowl, whisk oil, milk, and egg.

In a medium bowl, add tapioca flour, salt, and frozen cheeses and gently fold to combine. Gradually pour the wet mixture into the dry ingredients, folding until incorporated. Using an ice-cream scoop, scoop the dough into balls.

Place the balls onto the prepared baking sheet. Bake for 20 minutes, until golden and puffed. Serve immediately.

IN GOOD STOCK *The kitchen pantry is at the heart of every meal. It is where ideas are formed and creativity is born. Always have a well-stocked and organized cupboard, keeping the most used items readily available.*

MILK BREAD

This soft and fluffy milk bread practically melts in your mouth! Sweet and buttery, it's perfect for sandwiches or toast or just tearing into as a snack.

DOUGH

- ½ cup + 2 Tbsp milk (divided)
- 2 tsp instant yeast
- 3 cups all-purpose flour (divided), plus extra for dusting
- 1 egg
- ⅓ cup sugar
- 2 tsp milk powder
- 1 tsp salt
- ⅓ cup (⅔ stick) butter, room temperature and cubed, plus extra for greasing

FINISHING

- 1 egg

DOUGH Warm 2 tablespoons of milk in a small saucepan over low heat, then add yeast. Set aside.

In a separate small saucepan, combine ½ cup of milk and ¼ cup of flour and cook over medium-low heat until a paste forms.

Transfer the paste to a stand mixer fitted with a hook attachment, then add the remaining 2¾ cups of flour. Stir in egg, sugar, milk powder, and the yeast mixture. Mix on low speed until a shaggy dough forms. Add salt and mix on medium speed.

Add butter, one piece at a time, mixing on high speed until the dough pulls away from the sides of the bowl.

Transfer the dough to a large greased bowl, then set aside to proof in a warm area for 1–2 hours, until doubled in size.

Turn the dough onto a lightly floured surface and punch it down. Roll the dough flat, then roll it into a log and place on a greased baking sheet. Cover and proof for 1 hour.

FINISHING Preheat oven to 375°F.

Meanwhile, whisk egg and 1 tablespoon of water in a small bowl. Brush egg wash over the top of the dough. Bake the dough for 35–40 minutes, until golden brown.

SERVES **4** / PREP: **5** MINUTES / COOK TIME: **10** MINUTES

SOURDOUGH TARTINE

Ah, sourdough! Pile it high with fresh, seasonal ingredients, and you've got yourself a tartine that's both simple and elegant. It's my go-to for a satisfying lunch or a light snack — rustic, wholesome, and downright delicious.

TARTINE BASE
¼ cup butter
6 cloves garlic
12 sprigs thyme
4 (½-inch) slices day-old sourdough
Salt and black pepper, to taste

PAIRING Pinot Gris

TARTINE BASE Melt butter in a large cast-iron skillet over medium heat. Add garlic and thyme and sauté for 1 minute, until fragrant. Working in batches if necessary, add sourdough to the pan. Press down with the back of a spoon to ensure full contact is being made. Cook for 2–4 minutes, until golden brown, and flip. Continuously baste the top of the bread until a golden crust has formed and the bottom side is toasted.

Discard thyme. Season with salt and pepper.

TOPPINGS Tartines are an elegant canvas for creativity, offering endless possibilities for toppings that cater to every taste. Whether you crave savory, fresh, or indulgent, these combinations showcase the best of bold flavors and simple sophistication.

Mushroom and Feta
Tomato and Burrata Cheese
Avocado and Soft Poached Egg
Cream Cheese and Smoked Salmon
Muddled Berries (page 175) and Chantilly Cream (Simmer the muddled berries for 12–15 minutes, until thick and jammy.)

SERVES **8** / PREP: **15** MINUTES + **45** MINUTES FREEZING AND COOLING TIME / COOK TIME: **20–25** MINUTES

SMOKED GOUDA AND JALAPEÑO CORNBREAD

This is no ordinary recipe — it's an experience. Transform traditional cornbread with the rich, smoky creaminess of gouda, and double down on the heat with the addition of both fresh and pickled jalapeños. Ancho pepper and cayenne powder give a deep, earthy kick, while the buttery crust adds the perfect finishing touch. It's a match made in heaven with barbecue meat, but it works equally well with a hearty stew. Either way, this cornbread is possibly the star of the table.

INGREDIENTS

1½ cups grated smoked gouda
2⅓ cups cornmeal, plus extra for sprinkling
Butter, for greasing
1⅔ cups all-purpose flour
1 Tbsp brown sugar
1 Tbsp baking powder
1 tsp ancho pepper powder (see Note on page 76)
1 tsp salt
¾ tsp baking soda
¼ tsp black pepper
¼ tsp cayenne powder
¼ tsp ground cumin
¼ cup (½ stick) butter, softened, plus extra for brushing
1 Tbsp molasses
3 Tbsp honey
3 eggs
2⅓ cups buttermilk
1 Tbsp chopped pickled jalapeños
1 Tbsp chopped jalapeños
Maldon Salt, for sprinkling

PAIRING Bulleit Bourbon

In a small bowl, place gouda and toss it with a sprinkle of cornmeal. Freeze for 30 minutes.

Preheat oven to 375°F. Line a 13 × 9½-inch baking pan with parchment paper, then grease.

In a large bowl, sift together all the dry ingredients. In a medium bowl, whisk all the wet ingredients. Gradually mix the wet ingredients into the dry ingredients. Fold in the frozen gouda and both types of jalapeños, using a spatula. Pour the batter into the prepared baking pan. The batter should be no more than 1 inch deep in the pan.

Bake for 20–25 minutes, until golden brown. Set aside for 15 minutes, then invert onto a cooling rack.

In a small saucepan over low heat, melt butter for brushing. Brush onto cornbread, then sprinkle with Maldon Salt. Serve warm.

MAKES **1** LOAF / PREP: **30** MINUTES + **1** HOUR RISING TIME / COOK TIME: **25–35** MINUTES

GARLIC PULL-APART BREAD

This pull-apart bread is a garlic lover's dream: rich, buttery, and packed with layers of flavor in every bite. The soft, fluffy dough encases a mouthwatering garlic butter filling, which melts into the bread as it bakes, creating a perfect balance of savory and cheesy goodness.

INGREDIENTS

2 cups grated Parmesan
1 Tbsp garlic powder
1 Tbsp onion powder
1 Tbsp chopped parsley
1 tsp black pepper
1 tsp salt
½ tsp paprika
½ tsp cayenne powder
½ cup (1 stick) butter, softened, plus extra for greasing
1 quantity Milk Bread dough (page 57), prepared up to end of first proof

PAIRING Moretti beer

In a medium bowl, combine all ingredients except the dough and mix well to form a paste.

Roll the butter mixture into 8 small balls, each about 1 inch in diameter. Place them in the fridge to harden.

Grease a 10-inch square baking pan. Shape the dough around each of the hardened butter balls and roll into balls. Place the dough balls snugly together in the prepared baking pan. Set aside to rise for 1 hour in a warm place, until doubled in size.

Meanwhile, preheat oven to 350°F.

Bake for 25-35 minutes, until golden brown and cooked through.

SERVES **4** / PREP: **45** MINUTES + **2½** HOURS PROOFING AND RESTING TIME / COOK TIME: **1⅓** HOURS

POPPY AND NIGELLA SEED NAAN

This naan brings authentic flavor straight to your kitchen — no tandoor needed! The combination of spices and seeds deepens the flavor and gives the bread a satisfying crunch. With its soft, buttery texture and aromatic seasoning, this naan is perfect for scooping up curries or enjoying on its own when brushed with melted butter.

DOUGH

3½ cups all-purpose flour, plus extra for dusting
1¼ tsp salt
1 cup beer
2 Tbsp Greek yogurt
1 Tbsp honey
2¼ tsp active dry yeast

ROASTED GARLIC

10 cloves garlic, crushed
3 Tbsp butter, melted (divided)
Pinch of salt

SEASONED BUTTER

¼ cup (½ stick) butter, softened
2 tsp flaky sea salt
2 tsp nigella seeds
1 tsp poppy seeds

ASSEMBLY

Dough (see here)
Roasted Garlic (see here)
Seasoned Butter (see here)
1 Tbsp finely chopped cilantro, for sprinkling

DOUGH In a stand mixer fitted with a hook attachment, sift together flour and salt.

In a small bowl, whisk beer, yogurt, honey, and yeast. Set aside in a warm spot for 10 minutes, until yeast is activated and the mixture begins to bubble.

Add the wet mixture to the flour and salt. Mix on low speed for 3–4 minutes, until the dough comes together. Increase the speed to medium and knead for another 5–10 minutes, until the dough has a smooth surface and is no longer sticky.

Transfer the dough to a floured surface and knead by hand for another 15 minutes. The dough should stretch without tearing and have a smooth, elastic surface. Place the dough in a large greased bowl, cover with plastic wrap, and proof in a warm spot (around 81°F) for 2 hours, until doubled in size.

ROASTED GARLIC Meanwhile, preheat oven to 350°F.

Wrap garlic cloves, 1 tablespoon of butter, and salt in aluminum foil. Place on a baking sheet and roast for 30 minutes. Cool, then finely chop.

Brush the remaining 2 tablespoons of butter over top of roasted garlic.

SEASONED BUTTER Combine all ingredients in a small bowl and mix well.

ASSEMBLY Punch down the dough to release air bubbles. Divide it into 8 equal portions. Shape each into a ball, cover, and set aside to rest at room temperature for 30 minutes.

Preheat a nonstick grill or cast-iron skillet over high heat.

Roll or stretch each dough ball into a triangular shape. Place one in the pan and cook for 2–3 minutes, until the bottom develops a golden crust and bubbles form on the surface. Flip and cook for another 2–3 minutes, until the other side is charred in spots and cooked through. Repeat with the remaining dough balls.

With a fork, mash garlic into seasoned butter. While the naan is still warm, brush it generously with the garlic-seasoned butter mixture. Repeat with the remaining naan. Sprinkle with cilantro and serve immediately.

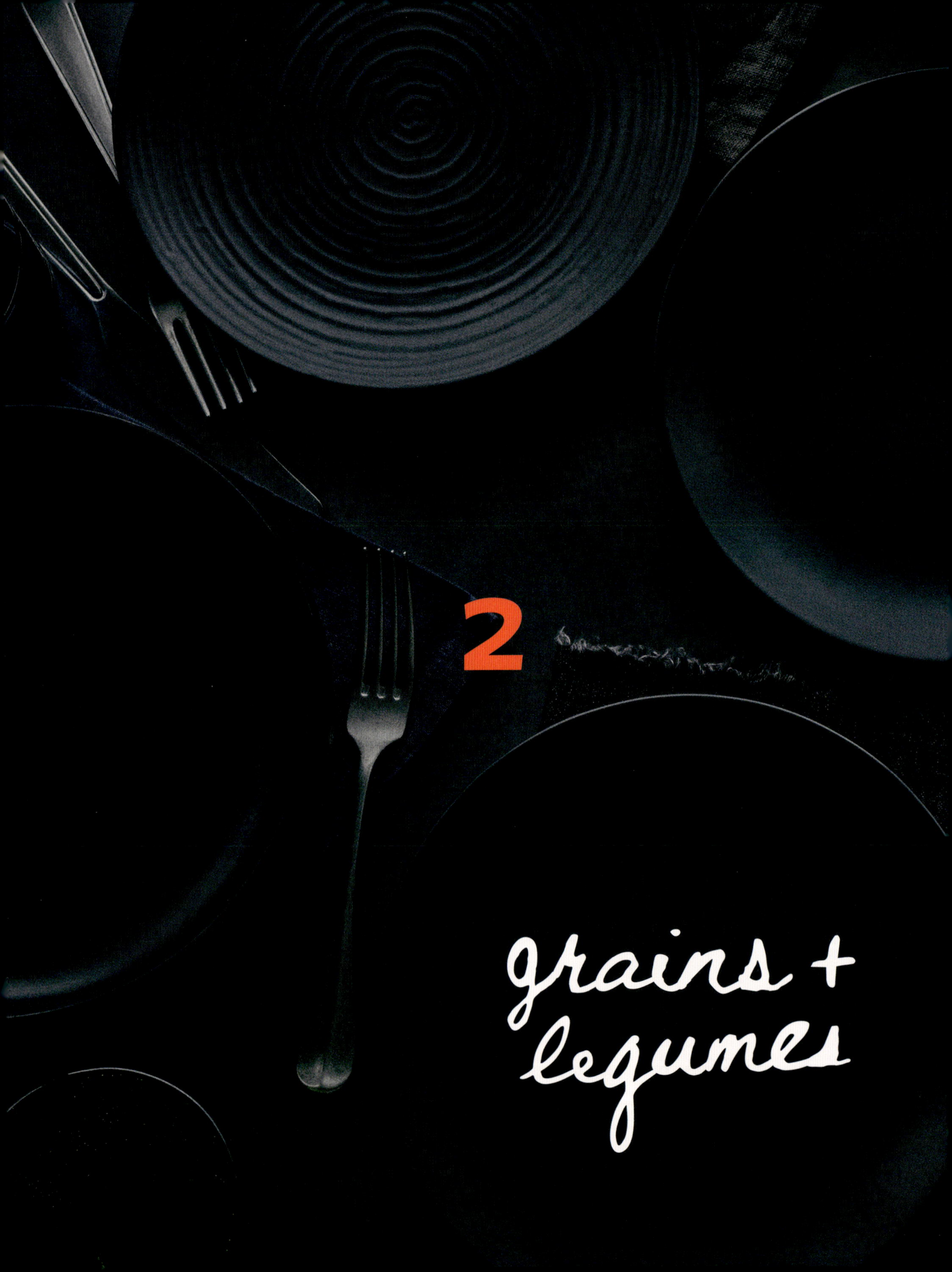

2

grains + legumes

Whether you're crafting a fluffy pilaf, hearty stew, or creamy risotto, the right water-to-grain ratios, cooking times, and techniques are key to a perfectly prepared grain dish. This table provides an easy-to-reference guide, ensuring every grain is cooked to perfection for your next meal!

grain guide

GRAIN	QTY	WATER	COOK TIME	COOK METHOD	USAGE
BASMATI RICE	2 CUPS	3 CUPS	18 MINUTES	STOVE TOP: STEAM	PILAF, BIRYANI
CAROLINA GOLD RICE	2 CUPS	4 CUPS	18–22 MINUTES	STOVE TOP: STEAM	PILAF, FRIED RICE
JASMINE RICE	2 CUPS	3 CUPS	30 MINUTES	RICE COOKER	COCONUT PILAF, POKE
SHORT-GRAIN RICE	2 CUPS	2 CUPS	30 MINUTES	STOVE TOP: STEAM	FRIED RICE, RICE CAKE
SUSHI RICE	2 CUPS	2 CUPS	50 MINUTES	RICE COOKER	SUSHI, POKE
WILD RICE	2 CUPS	8 CUPS	40–45 MINUTES	STOVE TOP: BOIL	PILAF, CRACKERS
BROWN RICE	2 CUPS	2 CUPS	40–45 MINUTES	STOVE TOP: BOIL	PILAF
BARLEY	3 CUPS	12 CUPS	30–40 MINUTES	STOVE TOP: BOIL	RISOTTOS, STEWS
FARRO	3 CUPS	12 CUPS	40–45 MINUTES	STOVE TOP: BOIL	SOUPS, SALADS, STEWS
FREEKEH	3 CUPS	12 CUPS	40–45 MINUTES	STOVE TOP: BOIL	SALADS, STEWS
OLD-FASHIONED OATS	2 CUPS	4 CUPS	8–12 MINUTES	STOVE TOP: COOK	PORRIDGE
QUINOA	3 CUPS	8 CUPS	12–15 MINUTES	STOVE TOP: BOIL	SALADS

OLD-FASHIONED APPLE AND BLUEBERRY OATMEAL

With the comforting heartiness of old-fashioned oats, the sweetness of apples, the tartness of blueberries, and a drizzle of maple syrup, this breakfast powerhouse is a balancing act between indulgence and nutrition. It is the ideal way to fuel your morning.

OATMEAL
2 apples, cored and diced
2 Tbsp brown sugar
1 tsp ground cinnamon
1 tsp lemon juice
2 Tbsp butter
1½ cups old-fashioned oats
2 cups milk
1 cup heavy (35%) cream
Pinch of salt
¼ cup maple syrup
1 cup blueberries

TOPPINGS
Fresh fruit
Dried fruit
Nuts
Nut butter
Chocolate chips

PAIRING Sparkling brut—blanc de blanc

In a medium bowl, combine apples, brown sugar, cinnamon, and lemon juice. Set aside.

Melt butter in a large saucepan over medium heat. Add oats and toast them for 1 minute, until fragrant. Stir in milk, cream, and salt. Continue to stir while bringing the mixture to a boil. Reduce heat to medium-low and simmer for 8 minutes. Stir in the apple mixture and maple syrup. Cook for another 4 minutes, stirring frequently, until oats are softened and the mixture thickens. Fold in blueberries and remove from heat.

Serve hot with your choice of toppings.

JAMBALAYA

This jambalaya is a flavor-packed powerhouse that doesn't hold back. Spicy sausage, juicy scallops, and sweet crayfish come together with smoky spices and perfectly cooked rice for a one-pot dish that screams New Orleans. It's the kind of meal that turns any night into a celebration.

INGREDIENTS

1 Tbsp + 2 tsp peanut oil (divided)
2–3 smoked andouille sausages, casing removed and crumbled (½ cup)
1 onion, finely chopped
2 cloves garlic, finely chopped
1–2 stalks celery, finely chopped (½ cup)
1 red bell pepper, seeded, deveined, and finely chopped
1 jalapeño, finely chopped
3 sprigs thyme, leaves only
1 bay leaf
1 tsp white wine
Dash of Tabasco sauce, plus extra to taste
½ cup canned crushed tomatoes
1 tsp Cajun spice
1 tsp smoked paprika
8 scallops, cut into quarters
4 cups warm chicken stock, plus extra if needed
6–8 okras, sliced (½ cup)
½ cup Carolina Gold rice
4–5 oz crayfish tails
Salt and black pepper, to taste
1 Tbsp lemon juice
1 Tbsp cilantro, for garnish

PAIRING Spanish Tempranillo

Heat 2 teaspoons of oil in a Dutch oven over high heat. Add sausages and fry for 2-3 minutes, until crispy. Set aside.

In the same pan, heat the remaining 1 tablespoon of oil, then combine onion, garlic, celery, bell pepper, and jalapeño. Add thyme and bay leaf and cook for 3-5 minutes, until vegetables are tender. Deglaze with wine and Tabasco sauce, scraping the bottom of the pan to release any browned bits.

Stir in tomatoes, Cajun spice, and paprika. Add sausages and scallops and cook for another 2-3 minutes. Pour in stock and boil for 5 minutes. Reduce heat to medium-low. Add okras, cover, and simmer for 5 minutes. Stir in rice, cover, and simmer for another 10 minutes.

Arrange crayfish tails on top and cover. Reduce heat to low and steam for another 10 minutes, until rice is cooked. If rice is clumpy, add more stock. If the jambalaya needs thickening, reduce it over high heat for a couple minutes. The final dish should be moist but firm enough to eat with a fork.

Discard bay leaf. Season with salt, pepper, lemon juice, and Tabasco sauce. Garnish with cilantro and serve hot.

LEMONGRASS AND COCONUT JASMINE RICE

This isn't your average rice. Infused with fragrant lemongrass, fiery bird's eye chilies, and rich and creamy coconut milk, it's an aromatic, flavor-packed side that will elevate any meal. Holy basil, with its slightly spicy and anise-like flavor, adds a unique herbal note that ties the dish together.

INGREDIENTS

8 Tbsp coconut oil
2 cups jasmine rice
4 cups coconut milk
4 stalks lemongrass, smashed and cut into 2-inch segments
8 bird's eye chilies, halved lengthwise
40 leaves holy basil, stemmed
Pinch of salt, to taste
4 cups water

PAIRING Tsingtao Beer or Asahi

Combine all ingredients except water in a rice cooker. Add water. Set the rice cooker to the standard white rice setting or cook for 25-30 minutes, depending on your machine. (Alternatively, combine all ingredients in a medium saucepan. Bring to a gentle boil over medium heat, then reduce to low, cover, and simmer for 18-20 minutes. Remove from heat and let rest, covered, for 5-10 minutes.)

Fluff the rice gently with a fork and serve hot.

SERVES **4** / PREP: **5** MINUTES + **20** MINUTES SOAKING TIME / COOK TIME: **20–25** MINUTES

BASMATI PILAF

This fragrant pilaf is a celebration of pungent spices, infused with the warmth of cinnamon, cardamom, cloves, and golden saffron. Serve this elegant and flavorful accompaniment with a rich curry.

INGREDIENTS
2 cups basmati rice
2 Tbsp butter
10 black peppercorns
4 green cardamom pods
4 whole cloves
2 star anise
1 cinnamon stick
1 tsp cumin seeds
Salt, to taste
3 cups water
1 tsp saffron threads

Rinse rice under cold running water until the water runs clear, removing excess starch. Soak rice in cold water for 20 minutes, then drain thoroughly.

Melt butter in a medium saucepan over medium heat. Add peppercorns, cardamom, cloves, star anise, cinnamon stick, and cumin seeds and sauté for 30 seconds–1 minute, until fragrant.

Stir in drained rice and salt and toast for 2–4 minutes, until lightly fragrant. Add water and bring to a boil, stirring gently to prevent sticking. Reduce heat to low, then stir in saffron. Cover and steam for 8–12 minutes. Set aside, still covered, for another 6 minutes.

Discard peppercorns, cardamom, cloves, star anise, and cinnamon. Fluff the rice gently with a fork and serve hot.

DAAL MAKHANI

Daal makhani is classic North Indian comfort food celebrated for its creamy texture and smoky flavors. Slow-cooked black lentils and kidney beans are enriched with butter, ghee, spices, and *tadka* — perfect for cozy dinners. Tadka, a traditional Indian flavoring technique, has spices and aromatics flash-fried in hot fat, then added to a dish at the last minute. When preparing a tadka, do not use any fat that will burn at high temperatures, and be sure to quickly remove the tadka from the heat once it's done cooking. Overcooking the tadka will burn the essence.

DAAL

4 tomatoes, diced
3 cloves garlic, roughly chopped
1 onion, roughly chopped (1 cup)
1 cup black lentils, soaked overnight
1 cup red kidney beans, soaked overnight
3 bay leaves
3 green cardamom pods
3 black cardamom pods
2 star anise
1 cinnamon stick
¼ cup ghee
1 tsp salt
4 L (16 cups) water

TADKA

¼ cup (½ stick) butter
4 cloves garlic, finely chopped
1 Tbsp ginger, finely chopped
2 tsp Kashmiri mirch (see Note) or paprika
2 tsp ground cumin
1 tsp ground coriander
1 tsp garam masala
2 tsp tomato paste

ASSEMBLY

Tadka (see here)
Daal (see here)
Salt and black pepper, to taste
1 tsp butter, room temperature, for garnish
1 tsp finely chopped cilantro, for garnish (optional)
1 tsp ginger, cut into matchsticks, for garnish

PAIRING Australian Grenache

DAAL In a blender, combine tomatoes, garlic, and onion and purée until smooth.

Transfer to a Dutch oven. Add drained lentils and kidney beans and the remaining ingredients. Bring to a boil. Reduce heat to medium-low, cover, and simmer for 2-3 hours, until lentils are tender and the liquid is thickened.

Discard bay leaves, both types of cardamom pods, star anise, and cinnamon stick. Using an immersion blender, pulse 3 times only to help thicken the daal. Keep warm.

TADKA Melt butter in a small skillet over medium-high heat. Add garlic, ginger, Kashmiri mirch (or paprika), cumin, coriander, and garam masala and sauté for 30 seconds, until the aromas have been released and the mixture is slightly golden in appearance. Add tomato paste and cook for 45-60 seconds.

ASSEMBLY Stir tadka into daal and simmer for another 15-30 minutes. Season with salt and pepper.

Garnish with butter, cilantro (if using), and ginger. Serve hot.

NOTE Kashmiri mirch is a mild chili known for its vibrant red hue and subtle heat. It's a staple in Indian cuisine, perfect for curries, tandoori preparations, and marinades. You can find it at Indian grocery stores or online.

THE GRAIN GAME *Portion grains and legumes, such as rice or lentils, into preset quantities to reduce preparation time.*

SCOTTY'S FRIED RICE

Scotty's fried rice is a weeknight hero – quick, versatile, and restaurant worthy. Charred veggies, aromatic spices, and a savory soy sauce create bold flavor, topped with a luscious, runny egg. Comforting, smoky, and packed with umami, it's perfect for busy dinners or lazy weekends. The key is chilled, day-old rice that fries without clumping.

FRIED RICE
4 cups rice
3 Tbsp canola oil (divided)
1 egg
2–3 shiitake mushrooms, thinly sliced
2 scallions, thinly sliced
2 cloves garlic, finely chopped
1 small carrot, thinly sliced
1 small shallot, thinly sliced
¼ cup edamame
¼ cup bamboo shoots, thinly sliced
3 dried long chilies
1 Tbsp dark soy sauce
2 tsp sesame oil
¼ tsp black pepper
Salt, to taste
Pinch of MSG (optional)
1 cup bean sprouts
1 Tbsp butter
¼ tsp white pepper

ASSEMBLY
1 Tbsp canola oil
4 eggs
Fried Rice (see here)
2 scallions, thinly sliced, for garnish
Sesame seeds, for garnish
Chili oil, for garnish

PAIRING Chilled green tea or a crisp Sapporo Beer

FRIED RICE Chill rice in the fridge overnight.

Heat 1 tablespoon of canola oil in a wok over high heat until smoking. Quickly scramble egg until just cooked. (You want the egg to be just cooked and relatively dry to avoid making the rice soggy. Aim for perfect timing – cooked through but not overdone.) Set aside.

In a small bowl, combine mushrooms, scallions, garlic, carrot, shallot, edamame, bamboo shoots, and long chilies. Set aside.

In a separate small bowl, whisk soy sauce, sesame oil, black pepper, salt, and MSG (if using). Set aside.

Break apart chilled rice with your hands.

Heat the remaining 2 tablespoons of canola oil in the same wok over high heat until smoking. Add the vegetable mixture and sauté for 2 minutes, until slightly charred. Add rice, scrambled egg, and bean sprouts and toss to combine. Add butter and drizzle the sauce mixture along the wok's edges. Toss for 1–2 minutes, until rice crackles and absorbs the sauce. Finish with white pepper.

ASSEMBLY Heat canola oil in a large nonstick skillet over medium-high heat. Add eggs and fry, basting with hot oil, until whites puff and yolks remain runny.

Pack one-quarter of the fried rice into a bowl, press gently, and invert onto a plate. Repeat with the 3 other servings. Top with fried eggs, then garnish with scallions, sesame seeds, and chili oil. Serve immediately.

BUY BULK *Buy legumes and grains in bulk, and store them in airtight containers to block out humidity or moisture, which can cause them to sprout!*

SHROOM RISOTTO

This isn't just risotto — it's a full-on flavor bomb. Earthy mushrooms team up with creamy, velvety rice to deliver a lavish and indulgent dish. Whether you're flexing your kitchen skills or in the mood for something ridiculously good, this risotto is the ultimate statement meal.

INGREDIENTS

2 Tbsp butter (divided)
4 cups mushrooms, cleaned and trimmed
3 cloves garlic, finely chopped (divided)
1 Tbsp finely chopped shallots (divided)
5 sprigs thyme (divided)
1 Tbsp red wine
Salt and black pepper, to taste
3 cups arborio rice
1 bay leaf
¼ cup white wine
6 cups hot vegetable stock
2 Tbsp grated Parmesan, plus extra shavings for garnish
Lemon juice, to taste
1 Tbsp finely chopped chives, for garnish
Extra-virgin olive oil, for drizzling

PAIRING Pinot Noir or Burgundy

Melt 1 tablespoon of butter in a medium cast-iron skillet over medium heat. Add mushrooms and roast for 4 minutes, until golden brown. Stir in half each of the garlic, shallots, and thyme. Deglaze with red wine. Season with salt and pepper, then set aside.

In a large dry skillet, toast rice over medium heat for 5 minutes, until it releases a nutty aroma. Add the remaining 1 tablespoon of butter and the remaining garlic, shallots, and thyme. Add bay leaf and sauté for 2 minutes, until the aromatics are tender. Deglaze with white wine.

Ladle stock into the rice mixture 1 cup at a time, stirring constantly and allowing each addition to absorb before adding more. Cook for another 15–18 minutes, until rice is al dente and the risotto is creamy. Stir in the mushroom mixture and grated Parmesan. Season to taste with lemon juice, salt, and pepper.

Discard thyme and bay leaf. Garnish with shaved Parmesan, chives, and a drizzle of oil. Serve immediately.

WINE RESCUE *If you have leftover wine unsuitable for drinking, blend red or white wine together for cooking purposes — if the wines haven't turned. Store the blend in an airtight bottle in the fridge for up to 2 weeks. For added depth of flavor, infuse the wine with herbs like rosemary, thyme, or sage.*

SERVES **4** / PREP: **15** MINUTES / COOK TIME: **25–30** MINUTES

ARROZ ROJO

Arroz rojo is a vibrant addition to any Mexican-inspired meal. Infused with tomatoes, chilies, and aromatic spices, it strikes the perfect balance of savory and zesty flavors.

INGREDIENTS

2 cups short-grain rice
8 Tbsp butter
4 small onions, finely chopped (2 cups)
8 cloves garlic, finely chopped
4 jalapeños, finely chopped
4 small tomatoes, finely chopped
2 small carrots, finely chopped (1 cup)
8 bay leaves
4 tsp ancho pepper powder (see Note)
4 tsp salt
4 cups chicken stock
2 cups water
4 Tbsp lime juice
8 Tbsp finely chopped cilantro, for garnish
Tapatío (see Note), to taste (optional)

PAIRING Modelo Especial

Rinse rice under cold running water until the water runs clear, removing excess starch.

Melt butter in a medium saucepan over medium heat. Add onions, garlic, jalapeños, tomatoes, and carrots and sauté for 3-4 minutes, until vegetables are softened.

Add rice, bay leaves, ancho pepper powder, and salt. Pour in stock and water. Add lime juice, then bring to a boil. Reduce heat to low and cover. Simmer for 8-12 minutes, until rice has absorbed the liquid. Remove the pan from the heat, then set aside for 6 minutes, still covered, for rice to steam.

Discard bay leaves. Fluff with a fork and garnish with cilantro. Add Tapatío (if using). Serve hot.

NOTES Ancho pepper powder, which comes from dried poblano peppers, is known for its smoky, slightly sweet flavor and gentle heat. Its earthy depth makes it perfect for enhancing sauces, stews, and spice rubs, adding richness without overpowering a dish.

Tapatío is a popular hot sauce with a tangy, spicy kick and a smooth texture that complements a variety of dishes. Made from red chilies, vinegar, and spices, it's known for its heat and vibrant flavor.

Look for both at larger grocery stores, Mexican specialty markets, or online.

SERVES 4 / PREP: 15 MINUTES + 8 HOURS SOAKING TIME / COOK TIME: 2¼ HOURS

FRIJOLES

Frijoles, or Mexican-style beans, are the soulful foundation of so many iconic dishes. Creamy, smoky, and packed with flavor, they're perfect as a side dish, a taco or burrito filling, or even the star of huevos rancheros. With deep roots in Mexican cuisine, frijoles prove that humble ingredients can create unforgettable flavors.

FRIJOLES
1 cup pinto beans, soaked overnight
½ onion
3 cloves garlic
3 bay leaves
2 chipotle peppers, canned in adobo sauce
1 cinnamon stick
1 Tbsp butter
1 Tbsp dried oregano
2 tsp salt
2 cups chicken stock

FINISHING
2 Tbsp butter
1 tsp cumin seeds
1 tsp adobo sauce (from chipotle peppers)
Salt, to taste
¼ cup chopped cilantro, for garnish

PAIRING Connor's Mezcal Sour (page 147)

FRIJOLES Preheat a grill or broiler to medium-high.

Drain beans, then rinse under cold running water. Set aside.

Add onion to the grill, cut side down, and char for 6 minutes until lightly blackened. Reserve.

In a large saucepan, combine all ingredients. Bring to a boil, then reduce to medium-low heat and cover. Simmer for 2 hours, until beans are tender.

Discard bay leaves and cinnamon stick. Transfer beans to a food processor and purée, adding the cooking liquid a little at a time to achieve a smooth, thick consistency resembling soft butter. Keep warm.

FINISHING Melt butter in a large skillet over medium heat. Add cumin seeds and toast for 1–2 minutes, until fragrant. Stir in puréed beans and adobo sauce. Season with salt.

Garnish with cilantro and serve warm.

3

vegetables

CUCUMBER AND KIMCHI SALAD

This vibrant, zesty salad combines the crisp freshness of cucumber and daikon with the bold, fermented kick of kimchi. Perfectly balanced with tangy, spicy, and savory flavors, this salad can easily shine as a side or be enjoyed as a light lunch. It's simple to prepare yet brimming with complex flavors that will tantalize your taste buds.

INGREDIENTS

1 cucumber, diced into 1-inch cubes (½ cup)
¼ daikon, diced into 1-inch cubes (½ cup)
1 Tbsp salt
1 tsp sugar
¼ cup sesame oil
2 Tbsp soy sauce
2 tsp gochugaru (see Note)
2 tsp gochujang (see Note)
1 tsp black pepper
¼ cup mandarin, peeled and segmented
½ cup chopped kimchi
3 Tbsp sliced scallions, plus extra for garnish
3 Tbsp cilantro leaves, plus extra for garnish (optional)
1 tsp white sesame seeds, plus extra for garnish
Daikon, sliced and punched into flower shapes, for garnish (optional)

PAIRING Tiger Beer

In a medium bowl, combine cucumber, daikon, salt, and sugar. Set aside for 15 minutes to release moisture. Drain.

In a separate medium bowl, combine oil, soy sauce, gochugaru, gochujang, and pepper. Add mandarin segments, kimchi, and the cucumber-daikon mixture and toss to coat. Stir in scallions, cilantro, and sesame seeds. Refrigerate for 10 minutes to marinate.

Garnish with scallions, cilantro (if using), sliced daikon (if using), and sesame seeds and serve cold.

NOTE Gochugaru and gochujang are the fiery backbone of Korean cuisine. Gochugaru, vibrant chili flakes, adds a smoky heat and nuanced depth to soups, marinades, and kimchi, while gochujang, a fermented chili paste, blends spice with a sweet-savory umami punch that's perfect for sauces, stir-fries, and dips. You can find these staples at Asian markets, well-stocked grocery stores, or online.

IN THE BAG *For enhanced flavor, vacuum-seal this salad in sous vide bags at 99 percent compression. The dressing will penetrate the vegetables more rapidly, creating a more intense flavor profile. The compression also slightly tenderizes the vegetables, while maintaining their satisfying crunch.*

GINGER-PEANUT PAPAYA SALAD

This peppy salad combines the tropical sweetness of green papaya, mango, and apple with the crunch of red cabbage and carrots, all brought together with a creamy, tangy, and slightly spicy ginger-peanut dressing.

SALAD
1 green papaya, cut into thin strips (3 cups)
1 green mango, cut into thin strips (1 cup)
1 green apple, cored and cut into thin strips (1 cup)
1 cup julienned red cabbage
1 carrot, cut into thin strips (½ cup)
1 cup bean sprouts
¼ cup cilantro leaves
¼ cup salted dry-roasted peanuts, crushed

DRESSING
2 cloves garlic, grated
½ cup tahini
½ cup peanut butter
2 Tbsp soy sauce
1 Tbsp sesame oil
1 Tbsp lime juice
1 Tbsp ginger juice
1 Tbsp honey
Black pepper, to taste

GARNISHES
Cilantro leaves
Crushed peanuts
Lime wedges
Red bird's eye chili, sliced
Crispy shallots

PAIRING Singapore sling

SALAD Combine all ingredients in a large bowl. Refrigerate until needed.

DRESSING Combine all ingredients in a blender and blend until smooth.

ASSEMBLY Pour dressing over salad. Using a rolling pin, gently pound the salad—just enough to marry the flavors without crushing the ingredients.

Garnish with cilantro, crushed peanuts, lime wedges, chili, and crispy shallots. Serve immediately.

TOMATO AND CIABATTA PANZANELLA

Panzanella is the quintessential Italian summer salad that brings together the best of seasonal tomatoes and bread. The tangy, slightly spicy dressing adds a balance of heat and acidity, while fresh basil and mozzarella complete this rustic dish. Whether served as a light meal or a side, it's the kind of salad that captures the essence of summer in every bite.

CROUTONS
1 Tbsp extra-virgin olive oil
2 cups cubed ciabatta
2 tsp dried oregano
1 clove garlic, finely chopped
Salt and black pepper, to taste

SALAD
2 cups cherry tomatoes, halved
¼ cup pearl onions, halved
2 Tbsp extra-virgin olive oil
Salt and black pepper, to taste

DRESSING
2 Tbsp extra-virgin olive oil
1 Tbsp finely chopped parsley
2 tsp white balsamic vinegar
1 tsp Calabrian chili paste
1 tsp lemon juice
Salt and black pepper, to taste

ASSEMBLY
2 heirloom tomatoes, chopped
Salad (see here)
Croutons (see here)
¼ cup Kalamata olives, pitted and halved
½ cup bocconcini mozzarella
Bunch of basil, leaves only, plus extra for garnish
Dressing (see here)
Salt and pepper, to taste
Shaved Asiago cheese, for garnish

PAIRING Lambrusco

CROUTONS Preheat oven to 400°F. Line a baking sheet with parchment paper.

Combine all ingredients in a small bowl and toss to mix. Spread the dressed bread cubes onto the prepared baking sheet and bake for 8–12 minutes, until golden brown and crispy. Set aside to cool.

SALAD Meanwhile, in a medium bowl, combine all ingredients. Place on a separate baking sheet, cut side up, and roast for 10 minutes with the ciabatta, until tender. Set aside to cool.

DRESSING In a small bowl, combine all ingredients and mix well. Set aside for 15 minutes for the flavors to meld.

ASSEMBLY In a large bowl, combine heirloom tomatoes, salad, croutons, olives, bocconcini, and basil leaves. Drizzle with dressing, gently toss, and season to taste with salt and pepper. Garnish with more basil and Asiago. Serve immediately.

FATTOUSH

Fattoush is a vibrant Lebanese salad that combines fresh vegetables like cucumber, tomato, and radish with crispy, toasted pita bread, offering a satisfying balance of crunch and flavor. The dressing, made with lemon juice, olive oil, and sumac, adds a bright, tangy kick that brings the whole dish together.

PITA CRISPS
1 Tbsp olive oil
½ tsp paprika
Salt and black pepper, to taste
2 pita breads, cut into ½-inch squares

SALAD
2 cups chopped romaine lettuce
½ cup thinly sliced red onion, separated into slivers (see Note)
¼ cup sliced radishes
¼ cup sliced watermelon radishes
¼ cup diced boiled beets
¼ cup sliced cucumber
¼ cup cherry tomatoes, halved
3 Tbsp chopped parsley, plus extra for garnish
3 Tbsp chopped mint, plus extra for garnish
3 Tbsp chopped dill, plus extra for garnish

DRESSING
¼ cup extra-virgin olive oil
3 Tbsp red wine vinegar
2 Tbsp lemon juice
2 tsp Dijon mustard
2 tsp sumac
Salt and black pepper, to taste

GARNISHES
¼ cup crumbled feta cheese
¼ cup Kalamata olives
Extra-virgin olive oil, for drizzling

PAIRING Black currant juice or mango soda

PITA CRISPS Preheat oven to 350°F. Line a baking sheet with parchment paper.

Combine all ingredients except pita breads in a small bowl. Add pitas and toss to evenly coat. Spread pitas on the prepared baking sheet. Bake for 14–18 minutes, until pita crisps are golden brown and crunchy. Remove from the oven and set aside to cool.

SALAD In a large bowl, combine all ingredients and mix well.

DRESSING Combine all ingredients except salt and pepper in a small bowl and whisk until emulsified. Season with salt and pepper.

ASSEMBLY Pour dressing over salad and toss gently to combine. Add pita crisps and toss again, ensuring everything is evenly coated. Garnish with feta, olives, herbs, and a drizzle of oil. Serve immediately.

NOTE To create slivers, cut the onion into rings. Cut the rings in half, and separate them to get strips of onion.

SALAD DAYS *Wash salad greens in ice-cold water and spin them dry. This crisps the vegetables and helps the dressing coat evenly.*

SALADS

Salads offer a vibrant way to nourish your body with vitamins, minerals, and anti-oxidants while inspiring endless creativity in ingredient combinations. Their variety in taste and texture makes them a versatile addition to any meal.

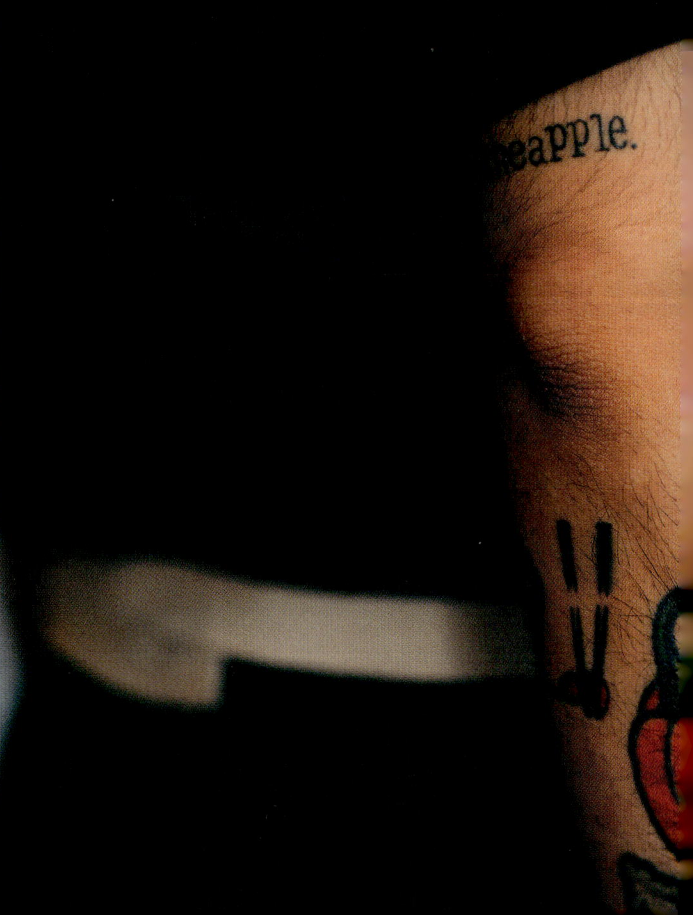

I aim to complement the dishes already on the table. For instance, with roasted chicken or braised pork, a hearty salad can make an ideal side. Similarly, a crisp salad with a citrus vinaigrette pairs beautifully with grilled fish or light pasta, providing a lively contrast.

If you've roasted a batch of root vegetables with rosemary and garlic, don't discard the trimmings! Use vegetable scraps, like carrot peels or onion skins, to infuse a vinaigrette. Blend them with rosemary, garlic, olive oil, and a touch of balsamic vinegar to create an aromatic dressing. The dressing ties in with the roasted vegetables, adding depth and harmony to the dish. Incorporating elements from the main course enhances the overall experience. Here's a simple guideline I like to follow for building salads.

GREEN UP YOUR GAME *Salads are a great way to use up excess ingredients like cheese, nuts, or dried fruit.*

Leafy Greens

These are your salad's base. Try romaine, spinach, or baby gem lettuce.

Crunchy Vegetables

Carrots, cucumbers, radishes, or sprouts add texture and freshness.

Fresh Herbs

Use herbs that complement the flavors of your main dish. Dill, parsley, or cilantro work well.

Croutons

These can be anything from tortilla strips to crispy pita chips or even fried brioche.

Fruits and Citrus

Add a bit of sweetness or acidity with fruits like oranges, strawberries, blueberries, or green apples.

Vinaigrettes and Dressings

Stick to a simple ratio of two parts fat to one part acid, with a dollop of mustard as a stabilizer. Dressings can range from the complex (chicken fat and apple cider vinegar, bacon fat and rice vinegar) to the simple (olive oil and lemon juice).

Seasoning

Reflect the essence of your menu with seasonings – perhaps a touch of cumin for an Indian-inspired salad or a sprinkle of sumac to bring out the zest of Mediterranean flavors.

SERVES **4** / PREP: **10** MINUTES / COOK TIME: **15** MINUTES

STREET-STYLE ELOTES

Elotes are street food royalty, and this recipe shows why! Each bite is a flavor-packed explosion: smoky, tangy, creamy, and irresistibly messy in the best way possible. Cut into wedges for a fun, sharable twist, these elotes are guaranteed to steal the spotlight at your next BBQ or family gathering.

CORN
4 ears corn, husked and trimmed of excess silk
¼ cup (½ stick) butter, softened
Zest of 2 limes
Pinch of salt

CREMA
½ cup Cotija cheese
2 tsp Tajín
1 tsp black pepper
1 cup mayonnaise
1 Tbsp chipotle peppers in adobo sauce
1 Tbsp lime juice

GARNISHES
Tajín
Lime zest
Chopped cilantro
Cotija cheese

PAIRING Michelada

CORN Using a sharp knife or a serrated blade for clean, precise cuts, slice each ear of corn in half lengthwise through the core once, then again, to create 4 wedges per ear. Place corn wedges on a towel to keep them steady and prevent them from rolling.

Bring a large pot of salted water to a boil. Prepare a bowl of ice water. Boil corn wedges for 4 minutes until about halfway cooked, then immediately transfer them to the bowl of ice water to cool for 60 seconds. Drain and set aside.

In a small bowl, combine butter, lime zest, and salt. Slather the mixture over corn wedges.

CREMA Whisk all ingredients in a large bowl. Set aside.

ASSEMBLY Preheat a grill to high heat.

Grill corn wedges for 4 minutes, until slightly charred and blistered, turning frequently for even cooking. Add hot corn to crema, then toss to coat.

Arrange corn on a platter. Garnish with a dusting of Tajín, lime zest, cilantro, and Cotija cheese. Serve immediately.

SERVES **4** / PREP: **15** MINUTES + **40** MINUTES STANDING AND CHILLING TIME / COOK TIME: **15–20** MINUTES

MOM'S SPINACH AND ONION PAKORAS

These crispy, spiced pakoras are a family-favorite snack that's perfect for starting a meal. This is my mom's recipe, so prepare to enjoy a taste of comfort. The batter requires soda water for that airy crunchiness.

INGREDIENTS

1 potato, thinly sliced with a mandolin
1 white onion, thinly sliced with a mandolin
2 cups spinach, roughly chopped
3 tsp salt (divided)
2 tsp chili flakes
1 cup chickpea flour
½ cup cornstarch
4 tsp curry powder
2 tsp carom seeds (*ajwain*)
½ cup soda water, chilled
Canola oil, for deep-frying
Chaat masala, for sprinkling
Caitlyn's Curry Ketchup (page 178) or your favorite dipping sauce, to serve

PAIRING Masala chai

Cut potato slices into thin matchsticks. In a large bowl, combine potato, onion, spinach, 1 teaspoon of salt, and chili flakes. Set aside for 10 minutes.

Squeeze out the excess moisture from vegetables. In a separate large bowl, combine chickpea flour, cornstarch, curry powder, carom seeds, and the remaining 2 teaspoons of salt. Add vegetables and toss to coat. Gradually pour in soda water, mixing until a thick, lumpy batter forms that holds its shape. Refrigerate for 30 minutes.

Pour oil into a deep fryer or deep saucepan and heat to a temperature of 375°F. Carefully lower small clumps of batter into the pan, taking care not to splash hot oil. Work in batches to avoid overcrowding. Deep-fry for 2-3 minutes, until the edges turn golden brown. Flip, then deep-fry for another 2-3 minutes, until golden. Using a slotted spoon, transfer the pakoras to a paper towel-lined plate to drain. Sprinkle immediately with chaat masala.

Serve with curry ketchup (or your favorite dipping sauce).

SERVES **4** / PREP: **15** MINUTES / COOK TIME: **50** MINUTES

SID'S CLASSIC TOMATO SOUP

This tomato soup is the epitome of comfort: smooth, velvety, and bursting with the kind of homemade flavor that makes you feel right at home. With just a few simple ingredients — ripe tomatoes, basil, and a touch of cream — it comes together into something truly satisfying on a chilly evening. This one's for you, bro.

SOUP
1 Tbsp butter, plus extra if desired
1 onion, finely chopped
2 cloves garlic, finely chopped
1 Tbsp finely chopped basil stems
1 Tbsp tomato paste
1 Tbsp white wine
4 vine-ripened tomatoes, chopped (2 cups)
2 tsp tomato powder (optional)
4 cups vegetable stock
½ cup heavy (35%) cream
1 small knob Parmesan rind
½ bunch basil, bundled in a cheesecloth sachet
Salt and black pepper, to taste

CROUTONS
4 slices sourdough bread, cut into large cubes
Olive oil, for drizzling
Salt and black pepper, to taste

ASSEMBLY
Soup (see here)
Croutons (see here)
Sliced mozzarella
Extra-virgin olive oil, for drizzling
Grated Parmesan
Basil leaves, for garnish

PAIRING French 75

SOUP Melt butter in a large saucepan over medium heat. Add onion and garlic and sauté for 8 minutes, until onion is softened and begins to caramelize. Stir in basil stems. Reduce heat if necessary to prevent garlic from burning.

Stir in tomato paste and cook for another 2 minutes. Deglaze with wine, allowing it to reduce until about three-quarters of the liquid evaporates. Add chopped tomatoes, tomato powder (if using), stock, and cream. Bring the mixture to a boil. Add Parmesan rind and basil sachet.

Reduce heat to medium-low, cover, and simmer for 30 minutes, until reduced by a quarter. Remove Parmesan rind and basil sachet.

Pour soup into a high-speed blender and blend until smooth and creamy. For a silky finish, add a small knob of butter. Season with salt and pepper.

CROUTONS Meanwhile, preheat oven to 400°F.

Place sourdough cubes on a baking sheet, drizzle with oil, and season with salt and pepper. Toast in the oven for 8–12 minutes, until golden brown.

ASSEMBLY Ladle soup into oven-safe bowls and top with croutons. Add mozzarella, drizzle with oil, and broil at medium heat until cheese is melted and bubbling.

Garnish with Parmesan and basil and serve.

SERVES **4** / PREP: **25** MINUTES + **9½** HOURS SOAKING AND CHILLING TIME / COOK TIME: **15** MINUTES

FALAFELS

Crispy on the outside and tender on the inside, this dish has earned the stamp of approval from our taste testers Alli and Raghab! Whether tucked into a warm pita or enjoyed as a snack, these falafels are the perfect balance of crunch and herby goodness. Alli and Raghab run Ceci Cela, the convenience store located in the same building as our restaurant. When a family meal isn't in the cards, Ceci Cela is always ready with a refreshing drink and a tasty bite to go.

INGREDIENTS

1 Tbsp baking soda
4 L (16 cups) water
2 cups dried chickpeas
3 cloves garlic, chopped
1 onion, roughly chopped
1½ cups chopped cilantro
1½ cups chopped parsley
1 large jalapeño, chopped
3 Tbsp white sesame seeds, toasted
2 Tbsp cumin seeds
2 Tbsp coriander seeds
1 Tbsp sumac
2 tsp cayenne powder
1 tsp salt, plus extra to taste
1 tsp black pepper
½ cup lemon juice
3 Tbsp tahini
4 tsp pomegranate molasses
Canola oil, for frying
Micro cilantro, for garnish
Sumac Tzatziki (page 167) or your favorite dipping sauce, to serve

PAIRING Buttery Northern California Chardonnay

In a large bowl, combine baking soda and water. Add dried chickpeas, ensuring there is at least double the amount of water to chickpeas. Soak overnight at room temperature.

Combine the remaining ingredients except oil in a separate large bowl, stirring until the mixture forms a paste. Drain chickpeas well, then add them to the bowl and mix.

Pass the mixture through a meat grinder set to medium coarseness until ground. Using a wooden spoon, mix thoroughly to ensure the flavors are evenly distributed. Chill the mixture for 30 minutes.

Transfer the mixture to a cheesecloth, then squeeze to remove any excess moisture. This step prevents the falafels from falling apart while frying.

Roll the chickpea mixture into 20 evenly sized balls, wetting your hands with water as needed to prevent sticking. Refrigerate for 1 hour, until firm.

Pour oil into a deep fryer or deep saucepan and heat to a temperature of 350°F. Carefully lower falafel into the pan, taking care not to splash hot oil. Work in batches to avoid overcrowding. Deep-fry for 6 minutes, ensuring falafels are mostly submerged in oil, until golden brown and crisp. Using a slotted spoon, transfer them to a paper towel-lined plate to drain. Season immediately with salt.

Garnish with micro cilantro and serve immediately with tzatziki (or your favorite dipping sauce).

MILK-FRIED CAULIFLOWER

Crispy and golden on the outside with a creamy, tender center, this whole-roasted cauliflower makes a stunning centerpiece. Braising it in milk infused with aromatic herbs and spices before breading and frying enhances its flavor and richness. The result is a beautifully seasoned dish that's perfect for sharing – if you can bring yourself to share it. ;)

BRAISED CAULIFLOWER
2 small heads cauliflower
3 cloves garlic
1 bay leaf
Sprig of thyme
2 tsp salt
1 tsp black pepper
1 tsp fennel seeds
4 cups milk

BREADING
3 eggs
1 tsp lemon-pepper seasoning
1 cup all-purpose flour
2 cups Italian breadcrumbs

ASSEMBLY
Braised Cauliflower (see here)
Breading (see here)
Canola oil, for deep-frying
Lemon-pepper seasoning, for sprinkling
Vadouvan spice powder (see Note), for sprinkling
Maldon Salt, for sprinkling
Parsley Aioli (page 172) or your favorite dipping sauce, to serve (optional)

PAIRING Cabernet Franc or Australian Shiraz

BRAISED CAULIFLOWER Combine all ingredients in a large saucepan, ensuring cauliflower is submerged. Bring to a boil. Reduce heat to medium-low and simmer for 6–9 minutes, until cauliflower is firm and only partially tender. Transfer cauliflower to a plate, then chill in the fridge until fully cooled.

BREADING Meanwhile, in a small, shallow dish, whisk eggs and lemon-pepper seasoning. Set up a breading station with separate large dishes for flour, the egg mixture, and breadcrumbs.

ASSEMBLY Discard bay leaf and thyme from cauliflower. Dust braised cauliflower with flour, dip it into the egg mixture, and coat it completely in breadcrumbs. Refrigerate breaded cauliflower for 30 minutes–1 hour to allow the coating to set.

Pour oil into a deep fryer or deep saucepan and heat to a temperature of 350°F. Carefully lower one breaded cauliflower into the pan, taking care not to splash hot oil. Deep-fry for 3 minutes, ladling hot oil on top to ensure even cooking. Turn over and deep-fry for another 3 minutes, until golden brown. Carefully transfer cauliflower to a wire rack set over paper towels to drain. Repeat with the second cauliflower. Sprinkle with lemon-pepper seasoning, vadouvan, and a pinch of Maldon Salt.

Cut into wedges and serve immediately with parsley aioli (or your favorite dipping sauce), if using.

NOTE Vadouvan spice powder is a fragrant, French-inspired curry blend that combines traditional Indian spices, such as cumin, mustard seeds, fenugreek, and turmeric. You can find it at specialty spice stores or online.

SERVES **4** / PREP: **20** MINUTES / COOK TIME: **35** MINUTES

GRILLED BRASSICAS WITH ROASTED GARLIC-LEMON VINAIGRETTE

Brassicas—including broccolini, Romanesco, and bok choy—are often overlooked, but when grilled, they become extraordinary. The smoky char from the grill enhances their naturally earthy flavors, while the roasted garlic-lemon vinaigrette adds a brightness that transforms them into a beautiful, balanced plate of depth and freshness. This dish is hearty enough to stand on its own yet light enough to complement any main course.

PISTACHIO CRUMB
⅓ cup shelled pistachios
Pinch of salt

BRASSICAS
Bunch of broccolini
1 head Romanesco
4 bok choy
Extra virgin olive oil
1 tsp chili flakes
Salt and black pepper, to taste

ASSEMBLY
Brassicas (see here)
Roasted Garlic-Lemon Vinaigrette (page 165)
Pickled peppers, for garnish
Pistachio Crumb (see here), for garnish
1 Tbsp finely chopped cilantro leaves
1 Tbsp finely chopped parsley leaves
1 Tbsp finely chopped mint leaves
1 Tbsp finely chopped dill

PAIRING Pomegranate mimosa

PISTACHIO CRUMB Meanwhile, combine pistachios and salt in a small skillet and dry-roast over medium heat for 6–8 minutes, until fragrant. Using a mortar and pestle, grind pistachios into a coarse crumb. Set aside.

BRASSICAS Preheat a grill to medium-high heat.

Bring a saucepan of salted water to a boil. Prepare a large bowl of ice water. Blanch broccolini, Romanesco, and bok choy in the boiling water for 1½ minutes. Drain, then transfer to the bowl of ice water and cool for 1 minute. Remove vegetables, then pat dry.

In a separate large bowl, toss blanched vegetables with oil and season with chili flakes, salt, and pepper. Grill until slightly charred.

ASSEMBLY Place grilled brassicas on a warm platter, drizzle generously with garlic-lemon vinaigrette, and garnish with pickled peppers and pistachio crumb. Combine herbs in a small bowl and sprinkle over vegetables.

WILT NOT, WANT NOT *Wilted, near-expired herbs can be dried in the sun (or dehydrated in a low oven), then chopped and frozen in ice cube trays with water. Add them later to soups, stocks, or sauces.*

NEW POTATOES WITH PAPRIKA

New potatoes, with their thin skins and waxy texture, are the perfect vessels for flavor, and when paired with the rich smokiness of paprika, they take on a vibrant personality. Roasting them until crispy gives them that perfect, irresistible crunch, making this dish a comforting favorite.

INGREDIENTS

Butter, for greasing
16 new potatoes
½ cup (1 stick) butter
8 cloves garlic
2 bay leaves
2 sprigs thyme
2 tsp brown sugar
4 tsp red wine vinegar
4 tsp paprika, plus extra for sprinkling
Salt and black pepper, to taste
Ramp Ranch (page 169) or your favorite dipping sauce, to serve

PAIRING Pisco Collins

Preheat oven to 425°F. Line a baking sheet with parchment paper, then grease with butter.

Place potatoes in a large saucepan and cover with cold salted water. Bring to a boil and cook for 15-20 minutes, until tender. Drain, then set aside to cool.

Melt ½ cup of butter in a small saucepan over medium heat. Add the remaining ingredients and stir until fragrant. Set aside.

Using the bottom of a skillet or the palm of your hand, gently crush each potato until it slightly bursts open yet retains its shape. Place potatoes on the prepared baking sheet. Brush them generously with the paprika-butter mixture, ensuring every potato is coated well. Roast for 18-20 minutes, until potatoes are crispy and golden on the outside.

Discard bay leaves and thyme. Transfer roasted potatoes to a serving dish. Sprinkle with paprika and season with salt and pepper.

Serve immediately with ramp ranch (or your favorite dipping sauce).

4

fish + seafood

ORANGE AND GINGER-CURED TROUT

This dish combines the citrusy zing of orange with the warm, pungent kick of ginger to create a cure that leaves the trout lively and bright. It's my go-to for a light, refreshing meal that still feels indulgent and gourmet. Add a creamy potato salad, fresh greens, and crispy bagel chips, and you've got yourself a winning combination.

INGREDIENTS

1 cup salt
1 cup sugar
⅓ cup brown sugar
2 Tbsp finely grated ginger
2 tsp coriander seeds, toasted and crushed
Bunch of dill, chopped, plus extra for garnish
Zest of 4 oranges, plus extra for garnish
Zest of 4 limes, plus extra for garnish
1 cup maple syrup, plus extra for brushing
¼ cup orange juice
¼ cup lime juice
2 skin-on trout fillets
Chopped chives, for garnish
Capers, for garnish
Potato salad, to serve
Fresh greens, to serve
Bagel chips, to serve
Sour cream, to serve

PAIRING Saint-Bris

In a small bowl, combine all ingredients except trout. Set aside.

Rinse trout under cold running water, then pat dry with a clean paper towel.

Place half of the cure in a large airtight plastic container. Place fish, skin side down, into the mixture. Then, place a layer of the curing mixture over the flesh. Refrigerate for 4 hours.

Rinse trout again under cold running water. Brush with maple syrup, then refrigerate for 24 hours to air-dry.

Using a sharp slicing knife, cut fish on the bias (diagonally), along the grain, into ⅛-inch slices. Start by slicing the head side of the fillet to ensure wider portions.

Carefully overlap fish on a serving dish. Garnish with orange and lime zest, dill, chives, and capers. Serve cold with potato salad, fresh greens, bagel chips, and sour cream on the side.

TUNA POKE WITH SESAME KEWPIE

Bright, fresh, and bursting with umami, this poke celebrates the best of top-quality ingredients. The velvety avocado and tender tuna are brought to life by a luscious, creamy sesame dressing.

INGREDIENTS

12 oz sashimi-grade yellowfin tuna, cut into ½-inch cubes
1½ Tbsp soy sauce
½ tsp wasabi
3 Tbsp Kewpie mayonnaise
1 Tbsp finely chopped jalapeño
1 Tbsp pineapple juice
¼ tsp sesame oil
Zest and juice of 1 lime
Salt and black pepper, to taste
¼ cup wakame seaweed, cut into thin strips
1 Tbsp macadamia nuts, toasted and chopped
1 Tbsp white sesame seeds, toasted
1 Tbsp black sesame seeds, toasted
8 cups steamed rice, to serve
1 avocado, sliced
1 Tbsp finely chopped scallions, for garnish
¼ cup cilantro leaves, for garnish
4 toasted nori sheets, cut into thin strips, for garnish

PAIRING Verdicchio

Place tuna in a medium bowl over another bowl filled with ice. In a small bowl, combine soy sauce and wasabi, then pour over tuna and gently mix. Refrigerate for 45 minutes to marinate.

Drain off any moisture that may have leached from tuna.

In a large bowl, combine tuna, mayonnaise, jalapeño, pineapple juice, oil, and lime zest and juice. Season with salt and pepper. Stir in wakame, nuts, and both types of sesame seeds.

Place the mixture over bowls of rice and add avocado slices. Garnish with scallions, cilantro, and toasted nori.

KATAIFI-WRAPPED MISO HALIBUT

This dish is a celebration of textures and flavors! *Kataifi* is a delicate, shredded phyllo dough, often used in Middle Eastern and Mediterranean cuisines to create a crispy, crunchy coating. Here, I've wrapped it around flaky halibut brushed with a savory, umami-hitting miso paste and fried it until golden and crispy.

INGREDIENTS

3 Tbsp salt
5 cups warm water
12 oz halibut, cut into 1 x 3-inch batons
½ cup miso paste
2 cups + 3 Tbsp clarified butter (divided)
1 (1-lb) box kataifi dough, divided into strands
4 roasted lemon wedges, for garnish
Chili Mayo (page 171), to serve

PAIRING Burgundian Chardonnay

In a large bowl, combine salt and water and stir until salt has dissolved. Reserve the brine in the fridge, until the liquid is completely chilled.

Add halibut to the brine and set aside at room temperature for 30 minutes to develop a firmer texture.

Remove fish from the brine, then pat dry. Lightly brush with miso paste. Set aside.

Heat 2 cups of clarified butter in a small saucepan over low heat, until just liquid.

Line a baking sheet with parchment paper. Place an even layer of kataifi strands onto the prepared sheet, then generously brush them with clarified butter. Place a fish portion over kataifi, then fold kataifi over and roll it around fish, until the entire fish is wrapped. Refrigerate until butter has solidified.

Heat the remaining 3 tablespoons of clarified butter in a large skillet over medium heat. Place fish in the pan away from yourself to avoid splatter. Cook for 2 minutes on each side, until golden brown. Baste fish, occasionally, to ensure even cooking.

Serve immediately with roasted lemon wedges and chili mayo.

SERVES **4** / PREP: **20** MINUTES + **2 ½** HOURS OF MARINATING, AIR-DRYING, AND CHILLING TIME / COOK TIME: **15** MINUTES

IPA-BATTERED COD

This IPA-battered fish is everything you crave in a pub classic — only better. Paired with a rich, spice-infused vadouvan tartar sauce, this dish is here to shake up your idea of what fish and chips should be.

INGREDIENTS

4 cod fillets
⅓ cup + 1 tsp salt (divided), plus extra to taste
1 cup all-purpose flour, plus extra for dredging
¼ cup rice flour
⅓ cup cornstarch
2 cups IPA beer
Canola oil, for deep-frying
Flaky salt, to taste
Malt vinegar powder, for dusting, or malt vinegar in a spray bottle, for spraying
Vadouvan Tartar Sauce (page 172), to serve
Lemon wedges, to serve

PAIRING English ale or Boddington Beer

Trim cod fillets of any excess sinew or bones, then set aside.

In a large bowl, whisk ⅓ cup of salt and ice water. Submerge fillets in the brine for 1 hour in the fridge.

Remove fillets and set aside to air-dry for 1 hour. This helps the batter adhere to the fish.

Meanwhile, in a large bowl, sift together both flours, cornstarch, and 1 teaspoon of salt. Whisk in beer until smooth. Refrigerate for 30 minutes to aerate and chill.

Pour oil into a deep fryer or deep saucepan and heat to a temperature of 350°F. Season fish with salt, then lightly dredge in flour. Dredge in the chilled batter, ensuring both sides are generously coated. Carefully lower fish into the pan, taking care not to splash hot oil. Gently move fish back and forth to prevent it from sticking to the bottom of the pan. Deep-fry for about 8 minutes, until fish is golden brown and crispy. Transfer to a wire rack set over paper towels and set aside for 2 minutes. Immediately season with flaky salt and dust with malt vinegar powder (or spray with malt vinegar).

Serve with a side of vadouvan tartar sauce and lemon wedges.

SERVES **4** / PREP: **20** MINUTES / COOK TIME: **1–1¼** HOURS

ACADIAN CHOWDER

It's a battle of the chowders! This recipe might ruffle some feathers, but let's be real: in any East Coast vs. West Coast showdown, I believe the East Coast takes the crown every time. Nothing quite compares to a classic boardwalk chowder. It's the ultimate way to cozy up by the shore on a crisp Acadian afternoon.

INGREDIENTS

2 cups fish stock
½ cup clam juice
¼ cup milk
Pinch of salt
2 potatoes, finely chopped (divided)
¼ cup finely chopped smoked bacon
3 Tbsp clarified butter (divided)
2 Tbsp finely chopped onions
2 Tbsp finely chopped celery
1 bay leaf
2 cloves garlic, finely chopped
1 Tbsp white wine
¼ cup whipping cream
Sprig of thyme
1 cup canned clams, chopped
¼ cup canned smoked clams
¼ cup bay scallops
¼ cup Nordic shrimp
1 tsp lemon juice
Salt and black pepper, to taste
White pepper, to taste
1 Tbsp chopped chives, for garnish
Toasted panko breadcrumbs, for garnish
Grilled bread, to serve

PAIRING Dry Chardonnay

In a medium saucepan, combine stock, clam juice, milk, and pinch of salt. Add half of the potatoes and boil for 8 minutes, until parboiled. Using a slotted spoon, transfer potatoes to a small plate and reserve.

Meanwhile, add bacon to a large saucepan and fry over low heat for 6–7 minutes, until crispy. Remove bacon and set aside.

In the same pan with the rendered bacon fat, combine 1 tablespoon of clarified butter, onions, celery, bay leaf, and garlic. Add 1 teaspoon of water and sauté over medium heat for 6–8 minutes, until vegetables are tender. Add wine and deglaze.

Add the stock mixture and whipping cream. Simmer for 30 minutes, until reduced by a quarter. Add the other half of the potatoes and thyme and simmer for 10–12 minutes, until tender. Discard bay leaf and thyme.

Transfer the chowder to a high-powered blender and blend until smooth. Strain, then return the chowder to the pan. Add seafood and simmer for 5 minutes over medium heat, until seafood is poached. Add the reserved potatoes. Season with lemon juice, salt, and both types of pepper. Reduce heat to low. Do not boil the chowder; otherwise, it may split.

Stir in the remaining 2 tablespoons of clarified butter, then garnish with bacon, chives, and toasted breadcrumbs.

Serve hot with grilled bread.

WILD GARLIC CLAMS CASINO

Clams casino are clams baked with a delicious topping of breadcrumbs, bacon, garlic, and herbs. The vibrant kick of wild garlic gives this recipe a bold twist!

INGREDIENTS

2½ lbs live Manila clams
¼ cup finely chopped bacon
2 Tbsp butter (divided), plus extra to taste
5 sprigs thyme
½ cup + 1 Tbsp white wine (divided)
1 Tbsp finely chopped shallots
1 Tbsp finely chopped wild garlic (ramp) stems
1 cup panko breadcrumbs
¼ cup grated Parmesan
1 Tbsp finely chopped parsley
1 Tbsp thinly sliced wild garlic (ramp) leaves
1 tsp chili flakes
Zest and juice of 1 lemon
1 Tbsp finely chopped chives, for garnish
Lemon wedges, to serve

PAIRING White Sancerre

Place clams in a large bowl and run ice-cold water over them for 15 minutes to filter out most impurities. Drain and scrub clean.

Fry bacon in a large skillet over low heat for 6-8 minutes, until crispy. Remove bacon and set aside.

In the same pan, combine 1 tablespoon of butter, thyme, and clams over high heat. Add ½ cup of wine. Cover, then steam for 5-7 minutes, until clams have opened. Discard any unopened clams. Transfer cooked clams to a large bowl, then set aside to cool at room temperature over a separate bowl of ice. Strain the liquid and reserve.

Once clams have cooled, shuck them. Reserve the half shells alongside clams.

Melt the remaining 1 tablespoon of butter in a medium skillet over medium heat. Add shallots and wild garlic stems. Add breadcrumbs and toast for 2-3 minutes, until slightly golden brown.

Transfer the mixture to a food processor. Add Parmigiano-Reggiano, parsley, wild garlic leaves, chili flakes, lemon zest, and bacon. Pulse until well mixed.

Season the reserved clam cooking liquid with the remaining tablespoon of wine and lemon juice.

Preheat a broiler to low heat.

To build the clams casino, take a half shell and place a clam inside. Spoon ¼ tsp of the cooking liquid into the clam shell, then cover with the breadcrumb mixture. Place a small pat of butter on top of each clam.

Place the built clams onto a small baking sheet, ensuring they are all facing upward. Pour the remaining cooking liquid onto the bottom of the tray, covering just an eighth of the clams. Broil for 4 minutes at low heat to toast breadcrumbs.

Garnish with chives, then serve hot with lemon wedges.

LIQUID GOLD *Don't skimp on the cooking liquid from the clams — it's packed with flavor and is perfect for dipping some crispy bread as a snack for the table. Side note: "Liquid gold" was an expression that chef Almir da Fonseca always used, and it definitely applies here.*

SERVES **4** / PREP: **20** MINUTES + AT LEAST **1** HOUR MARINATING TIME / COOK TIME: **5** MINUTES

TANDOORI SALMON YAKITORI

Imagine the smoky goodness of yakitori, paired with the fiery spices of tandoori – this is fusion like you've never tasted before! The salmon is perfectly tender, with a charred exterior that seals in all the bold flavors. This recipe is one of my absolute favorites for bringing some heat to the table!

SALMON IN TANDOORI MARINADE
1 (2–3-lb) salmon fillet, cut into 1-inch cubes
6 cloves garlic, finely chopped
1 small onion, finely chopped (½ cup)
¼ cup chopped cilantro
¼ cup finely grated ginger
2 Tbsp toasted chickpea flour
2 Tbsp Kashmiri mirch (see Note on page 72)
1 green bird's eye chili, chopped
1 tsp ground cumin
1 tsp ground coriander
1 tsp ground turmeric
1 tsp cayenne powder
1 tsp black pepper
1 tsp salt
¼ cup Greek yogurt
1 Tbsp lemon juice

SALAD
1 Tbsp lemon juice
1 Tbsp extra-virgin olive oil
1 tsp sumac
Salt and black pepper, to taste
¼ red onion, thinly sliced, soaked in ice water for 10 minutes
1 cup frisée (curly endive)
1 tsp finely chopped cilantro
1 tsp finely chopped parsley
1 tsp finely chopped mint

ASSEMBLY
Salmon (see here)
16 scallions, cut into 1-inch segments
Salad (see here)
Chaat masala, for sprinkling
4 lemon wedges, to serve

SPECIAL EQUIPMENT
Konro grill
Binchotan charcoals
6-inch bamboo skewers, soaked

PAIRING Soave

SALMON IN TANDOORI MARINADE Reserve salmon in a medium bowl over another bowl filled with ice.

In a blender, combine the remaining ingredients and blend until smooth. Pour the marinade over fish and mix well. Refrigerate for 1–24 hours.

Drain fish of excess marinade, then pat dry.

SALAD In a small bowl, whisk lemon juice, oil, sumac, salt, and pepper.

Drain onion. Combine onion and the remaining ingredients in a medium bowl. Add dressing and toss to coat.

ASSEMBLY Preheat a Konro grill with binchotan charcoals until the flames have dispersed and coals are smouldering. Place a cast-iron grill on top to heat up.

Skewer 3 salmon pieces per skewer, alternating with scallions. Grill for 2 minutes on each side, until the internal temperature of salmon reaches 135°F. Yakitori will continue to cook after they're removed from the grill.

Plate salad, then arrange yakitori on top. Sprinkle with chaat masala and serve with lemon wedges.

WASTE LESS, FEAST MORE *At the restaurant, preparing a family meal is an operational expense, so we maximize offcuts and trimmings to minimize waste and costs. You can do this at home. For example, save lemon rinds after juicing to make **agua fresca**, a light, fruity, non-alcoholic beverage. Add a generous amount of fruit and let the mixture steep for a few hours. Sweeten to taste with simple syrup (1 cup sugar: 1 cup water) and serve!*

fish.
the idea of
contact with the
paper bag first
you can wrap the fish in dry
and give
a wet
prefer,

BALTIMORE CRAB CAKES WITH OLD BAY REMOULADE

This recipe highlights the iconic flavors of the Chesapeake Bay region, where crab meat is a local delicacy. The use of Old Bay seasoning, a spice blend synonymous with Maryland cuisine, evokes the essence of the area's seafood culture, with its coastal charm and timeless connection to the water. Serve these at any gathering, and watch them vanish in a flash!

CRAB CAKE BATTER
¼ cup finely chopped red onions
¼ cup finely chopped celery
¼ cup finely chopped parsley
¼ cup finely chopped chives
2 cups panko breadcrumbs
¼ cup mayonnaise
1 Tbsp mustard
1 Tbsp lemon juice
1 tsp Old Bay seasoning
1 egg yolk
⅓ tsp salt
Black pepper, to taste
2 cloves garlic, grated
2 lbs jumbo lump crab meat, picked clean

PANKO CRUMBLE
1 tsp panko breadcrumbs
1 tsp Old Bay seasoning
1 Tbsp finely chopped parsley
Zest of 1 lemon

ASSEMBLY
4 tsp melted butter, for brushing
Crab Cake Batter (see here)
Panko Crumble (see here)
4 lemon wedges, to serve
Old Bay Remoulade (page 168), to serve

PAIRING Sicilian Carricante white

CRAB CAKE BATTER In a large bowl, combine onions, celery, parsley, and chives. Add breadcrumbs, mayonnaise, mustard, lemon juice, Old Bay seasoning, and egg yolk. Add salt and pepper and mix well.

Gently fold in garlic and crab meat, taking care not to break up the lumps. Refrigerate for 30 minutes.

PANKO CRUMBLE In a food processor, blitz together all ingredients.

ASSEMBLY Preheat oven to 450°F. Line a baking sheet with parchment paper, then brush with butter.

Using a large ice-cream scoop, portion the crab mixture onto the prepared baking sheet. Generously sprinkle panko crumble over each crab cake. Bake for 12-15 minutes, until crab cakes are golden brown, warm in the center, and break apart easily when pierced with a fork.

Serve immediately with lemon wedges and Old Bay remoulade.

SERVES **4** / PREP: **15** MINUTES + **15** MINUTES FILTERING TIME / COOK TIME: **25** MINUTES

SAN FRANCISCAN CIOPPINO

Seafood cookery is all about simplicity. You want to keep it light, bright, and zesty! The magic lies in preserving the delicate flavors of the fish; overdoing it will overpower its natural beauty. Fresh fish should have a clean, ocean-fresh scent—anything that smells off is a definite no-go. I've had my fair share of amazing meals in the Bay Area, but nothing has ever come close to the cioppino at Sotto Mare, which served as inspiration for this dish.

INGREDIENTS
2½ lbs live mussels
2½ lbs live littleneck clams
1 Tbsp olive oil
4 bay leaves
3 cloves garlic, finely chopped
1 shallot, finely chopped
1 tsp finely chopped parsley stems
1 cup white wine
3 cups canned crushed vine-ripened tomatoes
1 cup fish stock
2 tsp chili flakes
2 tsp paprika
1 tsp Old Bay seasoning
1 tsp dried oregano
¼ tsp fennel seeds
4 snapper fillets, cut into 2-inch pieces
12 bay scallops
12 jumbo shrimp, shelled, deveined, and tails intact
Salt and black pepper, to taste
1 tsp lemon juice
1 Tbsp parsley, for garnish
Tabasco sauce, to taste
4 slices grilled sourdough, to serve
4 lemon wedges, to serve

PAIRING Red Châteauneuf-du-Pape

Place mussels and clams in a large bowl and run ice-cold water over them for 15 minutes to filter out most impurities. Drain, then scrub clean.

Heat oil in a large stockpot over medium-high heat. Add bay leaves, garlic, shallot, and parsley stems and fry for 1–2 minutes, until golden.

Add mussels, clams, and wine. Cover and increase heat to high, then steam for 6–8 minutes, until mussels and clams have opened. Discard any unopened mussels and clams. Transfer the mixture to a large bowl and set aside.

To the same pot, add tomatoes and stock. Add chili flakes, paprika, Old Bay, oregano, and fennel seeds. Sauté for 10 minutes. Add cooked mussels and clams, snapper, scallops, and shrimp. Cover, then reduce heat to low and steam for 4 minutes, until fish and seafood are cooked. Discard bay leaves. Season with salt, pepper, and lemon juice. Garnish with parsley and finish with a few drops of Tabasco.

Serve with grilled sourdough and lemon wedges.

SERVES **4** / PREP: **20** MINUTES + **15** MINUTES CHILLING TIME / COOK TIME: **25** MINUTES

HONEYED WALNUT SHRIMP

Is it Chinese food or is it *Americanized* Chinese food? Either way, this dish is delicious. Crispy shrimp are coated in a sweet, sticky honey sauce and paired with crunchy, caramelized walnuts — what's not to love? Perfect for a dinner party or a weeknight treat, this recipe brings restaurant-style flavors right into your kitchen.

HONEYED WALNUTS
½ cup walnuts
1 egg white
2 Tbsp brown sugar
½ tsp curry powder
½ cup honey
1 Tbsp sugar
1 tsp salt

SHRIMP BATTER
16 jumbo shrimp, shelled, deveined, and tails intact
⅓ cup Shaoxing wine
5 Tbsp cornstarch
1 tsp baking powder
1 tsp salt
1 cup soda water
1 egg white

SHRIMP SAUCE
⅓ cup sweetened condensed milk
2 Tbsp Kewpie mayonnaise
2 Tbsp rice wine vinegar
2 tsp honey
¼ tsp sesame oil
Zest of 1 orange
Zest of 1 lime
Salt and white pepper, to taste

ASSEMBLY
Peanut oil, for deep-frying
Shrimp Batter (see here)
Shrimp Sauce (see here)
Honeyed Walnuts (see here)
2 cups finely shredded napa cabbage, submerged in ice water
Chili-Garlic Oil (page 176), to taste
Sesame seeds, for sprinkling
Scallions, thinly sliced, for sprinkling
Steamed rice, to serve

PAIRING Alsace-style Pinot Gris

HONEYED WALNUTS Preheat oven to 400°F. Line a baking sheet with parchment paper.

Bring a small saucepan of water to a boil. Add walnuts and boil for 2 minutes. Drain, then set aside.

In a small bowl, combine the remaining ingredients. Fold in walnuts. Spread the mixture in a single layer onto the prepared baking sheet. Bake for 9 minutes, until crispy and caramelized. Set aside.

SHRIMP BATTER In a medium bowl, combine shrimp and wine and mix well. Set aside.

In a separate medium bowl, sift together cornstarch, baking powder, and salt. Whisk in soda water until the batter is smooth.

Whisk egg white in a small bowl until frothy but not overmixed. (This is key for a light, airy batter!) Gently fold whipped egg white into the soda water mixture. Place the batter in the fridge to chill for 15 minutes.

SHRIMP SAUCE Combine all ingredients in a medium bowl and mix well. The sauce should be thick enough to coat the shrimp without dripping off. Set aside.

ASSEMBLY Pour peanut oil into a deep fryer or deep saucepan and heat to a temperature of 350°F. Dip shrimp into the batter. Carefully lower shrimp into the pan, taking care not to splash hot oil. Work in batches to avoid overcrowding. Deep-fry for 6 minutes, until golden and crispy. Using a slotted spoon, transfer fried shrimp to a wire rack set over paper towels to drain any excess oil.

Toss crispy shrimp in shrimp sauce. Fold in honeyed walnuts.

To serve, drain cabbage. Pat dry and arrange on plates. Top with honeyed walnut shrimp, drizzle with chili-garlic oil, and add a sprinkling of sesame seeds and scallions. Serve with steamed rice.

5

meat

SERVES **4** / PREP: **20** MINUTES + AT LEAST **2¾** HOURS MARINATING AND CHILLING TIME / COOK TIME: **40–45** MINUTES

CRISPY KOREAN FRIED CHICKEN

Crispy, crunchy, juicy — straight-up fire! This recipe elevates everything you love about golden fried chicken with a spicy glaze that hits all the right notes: sweet, savory, and fiery. Trust me, this isn't just fried chicken — it's an experience. The recipe calls for both potato starch and potato flour, each bringing unique qualities to the frying process.

MARINATED CHICKEN
1 Asian pear, grated (½ cup)
2 Tbsp finely grated ginger
8 cloves garlic, finely chopped
2 cups buttermilk
¼ cup grated onion
1 tsp gochugaru (see Note on page 81)
1 whole chicken, cut into 8 pieces

SAUCE
¼ cup soy sauce
3 Tbsp dark soy sauce
3 Tbsp gochujang (see Note on page 81)
1 Tbsp finely grated ginger
1 Tbsp finely grated garlic
Pinch of MSG
½ cup water
2 Tbsp honey
1 tsp cornstarch

DREDGE
1 cup all-purpose flour
1 cup rice flour
½ cup cornstarch
½ cup potato flour
½ cup potato starch
2 Tbsp baking powder
2 Tbsp onion powder
2 Tbsp garlic powder
Salt and black pepper, to taste

ASSEMBLY
Marinated Chicken (see here)
Dredge (see here)
Peanut oil, for deep-frying
Sea salt, to taste
1 scallion, thinly sliced on the bias, for garnish
Sauce (see here)
2 Tbsp sesame seeds, for garnish
Cucumber and Kimchi Salad (page 81), to serve

PAIRING Pinot Noir

MARINATED CHICKEN Combine all ingredients except chicken in a large bowl. Add chicken, cover, and refrigerate for 2-48 hours. The longer you marinate the chicken, the more flavorful and tender it will be.

SAUCE In a small saucepan, combine both soy sauces, gochujang, ginger, garlic, and MSG. Add water and mix well. Bring to a boil. Stir in honey, then simmer for 10-15 minutes, until reduced by a quarter.

In a small bowl, mix cornstarch and 2 tablespoons of cold water. Slowly pour the mixture into the sauce. Bring to a quick boil, then simmer until sauce is thick enough to coat the back of a spoon. (The consistency is known as *nappe*.) Transfer to a large bowl and set aside.

DREDGE Combine all ingredients in a large bowl and mix well.

ASSEMBLY Remove chicken pieces from marinade, then dredge pieces in the flour mixture and shake off any excess. Set aside on a wire rack in the fridge for 45 minutes so flour adheres to the surface of the chicken.

Pour oil into a deep fryer or deep saucepan and heat to a temperature of 350°F. Carefully lower chicken into the pan, taking care not to splash hot oil. Work in batches to avoid overcrowding. Deep-fry for 11 minutes, until golden brown and crispy and the internal temperature reaches 165°F. Using tongs, transfer chicken to a wire rack set over paper towels. Immediately season with sea salt.

Place scallion in a small bowl of ice water for 2 minutes. Drain.

Add fried chicken to the bowl of sauce and toss to generously coat. Transfer to a serving platter, then garnish with sesame seeds and scallion. Serve hot, with cucumber and kimchi salad.

SERVES **4** / PREP: **20** MINUTES / COOK TIME: **~1½** HOURS

THE BEST BUTTER CHICKEN

Butter chicken is irresistibly delicious with tender, succulent chicken bathed in a rich, creamy sauce that blends warm spices with a hint of sweetness. It's my go-to whenever I'm with a crowd or hosting a gathering – guaranteed to impress and bring everyone back for seconds! It also happens to be the favorite dish of our front-of-house server who has been with us since day one.

SPICE BLEND

2 whole cloves
2 black cardamom pods
2 green cardamom pods
1 Tbsp coriander seeds
1 Tbsp cumin seeds
1 Tbsp Kashmiri mirch (see Note on page 72)
1 Tbsp paprika
1 Tbsp garam masala

BUTTER CHICKEN

2 cups chicken stock
2¼ cups whipping cream (divided)
3 Tbsp butter
1 Tbsp honey
6 cloves garlic
1 green bird's eye chili
½ small onion, finely chopped
2 Tbsp finely grated ginger
2 Tbsp cilantro stems
2 Tbsp ghee
½ cup tomato paste
Spices (see here)
½ cup diced tomatoes
4 large chicken breasts, cut into 2-inch pieces
Salt and black pepper, to taste
Cilantro, for garnish
Basmati rice or warm Poppy and Nigella Seed Naan (page 63), to serve

PAIRING Dry Gewürztraminer or white Zinfandel

SPICE BLEND In a small saucepan, toast cloves, both types of cardamom, coriander seeds, and cumin seeds over medium-low heat for 1–2 minutes, until fragrant.

Combine all spices in a small bowl.

BUTTER CHICKEN Preheat oven to 400°F.

In a large saucepan, combine stock, 2 cups of whipping cream, butter, and honey. Bring to a simmer over medium heat.

In a blender or food processor, combine garlic, chili, onion, ginger, and cilantro stems. Blend into a paste.

Heat ghee in a large oven-safe saucepan or Dutch oven over medium-high heat. Add the aromatic paste and sweat for 7–9 minutes, until translucent and golden brown. Stir constantly to prevent paste from burning. Add tomato paste, spices, and tomatoes and cook for 4–6 minutes, until the raw flavor of tomato paste has dissipated. Add chicken and cook for 5–8 minutes, until it turns opaque.

Slowly pour in the stock mixture. (It's important not to rapidly add the mixture on a high heat; otherwise, the cream will split. The goal is to temper the liquid before adding it to the pan.) Season with salt and pepper. Bring to a simmer and cover. Place in the oven and bake for 1 hour, until cooked through.

Meanwhile, in a small saucepan, reduce the remaining ¼ cup of whipping cream to a tablespoon.

To serve, drizzle reduced cream into the butter chicken, then garnish with cilantro. Serve with rice (or naan).

SERVES **4** / PREP: **20** MINUTES + **8** HOURS SOAKING TIME / COOK TIME: ~**1¼** HOURS

THE GUNSLINGER'S TURKEY CHILI

I cook hearty cowboy turkey chili on an open fire whenever possible. It's the perfect make-ahead dish for gatherings. As it simmers, the flavor deepens and intensifies, making it a guaranteed crowd-pleaser — easy to prep, big on flavor, and sure to satisfy everyone at the table!

SPICE BLEND
1 bay leaf
1½ Tbsp ground cumin
1 tsp cayenne powder
1 Tbsp smoked paprika
1 Tbsp paprika
1 Tbsp garlic powder
1 Tbsp onion powder
1 Tbsp brown sugar

CHILI
2 Tbsp butter
2–3 slices bacon, chopped
3 cloves garlic, finely chopped
1 onion, finely chopped (1 cup)
½ stalk celery, finely chopped (¼ cup)
⅓ green bell pepper, seeded, deveined, and finely chopped
1 poblano pepper, finely chopped (¼ cup)
1 jalapeño, finely chopped
1 cup brewed coffee
Spice Blend (see here)
3 cups chicken stock
1 cup crushed tomatoes
1 Tbsp ketchup
2 tsp apple cider vinegar
1 tsp Tabasco sauce
1 lb ground turkey
½ cup red kidney beans, canned or soaked overnight
½ cup black beans, canned or soaked overnight
Salt and black pepper, to taste
Sour cream, for garnish
Grated cheddar, for garnish
Chopped scallions, for garnish
Cooked Carolina Gold rice, to serve

PAIRING IPA

SPICE BLEND Combine all ingredients in a small bowl and mix well.

CHILI Melt butter in a Dutch oven over low heat. Add bacon and cook for 6-8 minutes, until the fat is nearly cooked. Using a slotted spoon, transfer bacon to a plate.

Heat the rendered bacon fat in the same pan over medium heat. Add garlic, onion, celery, and peppers. Sauté for 4-5 minutes, scraping the bottom of the pan to release any browned bits, until vegetables are tender. Add bacon.

Deglaze with coffee and cook until the liquid is reduced by half. Add spice blend. Pour in stock, crushed tomatoes, ketchup, vinegar, and Tabasco sauce. Bring to a boil. Add turkey and break it up with a wooden spoon. Simmer, uncovered, for 45 minutes-1 hour, until flavors are melded. Stir occasionally to prevent the mixture from burning. Reduce heat if necessary.

Stir in both types of beans. Using a masher, muddle beans to thicken the chili. Beans hold a lot of starch and help to give a traditionally thick chili texture. Do not over-mash! Discard bay leaf. Season to taste with salt and pepper.

Garnish with sour cream, cheddar, and scallions. Serve with rice.

CANDY BACON

How do I express my pride as a Canadian chef without saying it? With this recipe. This candy bacon is a masterpiece, melding smoky, salty, and sweet flavors into an unforgettable treat. A 24-hour brine, a maple-infused cure, and a hint of everything seasoning for crunch make each bite a journey of unapologetically Canadian flavors. Perfect for breakfast, a gourmet sandwich topping, or simply snacking with a cold drink, this recipe is a must for bacon lovers. This candy bacon takes time and patience to prepare and cook, but the delectable result is absolutely worth every minute of effort.

BRINE
12 slices pork belly, skin removed
3 Tbsp brown sugar
2 Tbsp molasses
1 Tbsp black pepper
6 cups water
3 cloves garlic
3 whole cloves
¼ onion
2 bay leaves

PORK BELLY
1 cup brown sugar
½ cup salt
¼ cup maple syrup
1 tsp ground cinnamon
Pork belly from Brine (see here)

SPECIAL EQUIPMENT
Maple wood, for smoking

EVERYTHING SEASONING
1 Tbsp onion flakes
1 Tbsp granulated garlic
1 Tbsp black sesame seeds
1 Tbsp white sesame seeds
1 Tbsp poppy seeds
1 Tbsp flaky salt
1 tsp black pepper

ASSEMBLY
Pork Belly (see here)
2 Tbsp maple syrup mixed with 2 Tbsp honey, for brushing
Everything Seasoning (see here)

PAIRING Old-fashioned cocktail

BRINE Roll each slice of pork belly into itself and tie with butcher's twine. Set aside.

In a large bowl, combine brown sugar, molasses, and pepper. Pour in water, stirring until sugar dissolves. Add the remaining ingredients and stir. Add pork belly and submerge. Cover and refrigerate for 24 hours.

Remove pork belly from brine. Transfer to a wire rack set over paper towels and air-dry for 2 hours.

PORK BELLY Combine all ingredients except pork belly in a large bowl and mix well. Add pork belly and fully coat with the mixture, ensuring pork belly is evenly encapsulated. Cover and refrigerate for 24 hours.

Rinse pork belly under cold running water to remove any excess salt. Pat dry, then allow it to air-dry for another 24 hours. This helps develop a tacky surface, known as the "pellicle," which allows the smoke to better adhere to the meat.

Prepare a smoker with maple wood chips. Smoke pork belly on low heat for 4 hours, ensuring the temperature is low enough to avoid cooking or rendering the fat. Cool pork belly in the fridge until firm.

EVERYTHING SEASONING Combine all ingredients in a small bowl and mix well.

ASSEMBLY Preheat oven to 325°F. Line a baking sheet with parchment paper.

Arrange pork belly on the prepared baking sheet. Brush each slice generously with the maple syrup mixture and sprinkle with everything seasoning. Bake for 15 minutes, until caramelized and glossy. (Watch carefully to avoid burning the sugar coating.) Set candied bacon aside for sugars to harden and form a crisp glaze.

Serve.

SERVES **4** / PREP: **20** MINUTES / COOK TIME: **1½** HOURS

RICOTTA AND GUANCIALE RIGATONI WITH GREMOLATA

Rigatoni is smothered in savory guanciale tomato sauce, creamy ricotta, and zesty gremolata for a dish that's indulgent, smoky, and irresistible. This is OG Italian, perfect for a *capo*. (This also happens to be the name of a San Franciscan restaurant that inspired this recipe.) It's comfort food with a touch of sophistication, guaranteed to make you rethink your weeknight dinner routine.

SAUCE

3 Tbsp extra-virgin olive oil
¼ cup finely chopped guanciale
2 bay leaves
2 hot Italian sausages, casing removed and crumbled
2 cloves garlic, finely chopped
½ shallot, finely chopped
⅓ cup red wine
1 Calabrian chili
1 Tbsp dried oregano
2½ cups passata
Salt and black pepper, to taste
1 (3-inch) Parmesan rind
Bunch of 5 basil leaves, tied together with kitchen string
2 Tbsp sugar

RIGATONI

2 bay leaves
1 tea bag of Earl Grey or black breakfast tea, leaves only
1 Tbsp salt
5 cups uncooked rigatoni

SAUCE Heat oil in a large saucepan over medium-high heat. Add guanciale and bay leaves and sauté for 3–4 minutes, until the fat has rendered. Do not crisp meat. Transfer to a plate. Discard bay leaves.

Heat the rendered fat in the same pan over medium-high heat. Add sausages and sauté for 3–4 minutes, until browned. Transfer to the plate of guanciale.

Add garlic and shallot to the same pan and sauté for 1–2 minutes over medium heat, until fragrant. Stir in sausages and guanciale. Pour in wine and deglaze.

Add chili and oregano, then pour in passata. Season with salt and pepper. Bring to a simmer. Add Parmesan rind, basil, and sugar and gently simmer, uncovered, over low heat for 1 hour. Discard basil.

Season and adjust taste for sweetness, acidity, and salinity. Keep salt on the lighter side since gremolata and ricotta will be added to the baked dish.

RIGATONI Meanwhile, in a large saucepan, combine bay leaves, tea leaves, and salt. Pour in water and bring to a boil. Add rigatoni and cook for 9 minutes, until al dente. Do not overcook pasta; otherwise, it will turn mushy when baked.

Drain pasta, then transfer to a paper towel-lined baking sheet. Refrigerate until needed.

RICOTTA FILLING
1½ cups ricotta
¼ cup chopped parsley
¼ cup grated Parmesan
1 egg yolk
¼ tsp chili flakes
Black pepper, to taste
Zest of ½ lemon

BREADCRUMB GREMOLATA
1 clove garlic, finely chopped
½ cup panko breadcrumbs
1 Tbsp finely chopped curly parsley
Zest of 1 lemon
Salt, to taste

ASSEMBLY
Extra-virgin olive oil, for greasing and drizzling
Rigatoni (see here)
Sauce (see here)
Ricotta Filling (see here)
Breadcrumb Gremolata (see here)
Grated Parmesan, for sprinkling
Chili flakes, for sprinkling
Basil leaves, for sprinkling
Black pepper, to taste
Garlic Pull-Apart Bread (page 62), to serve

PAIRING Barolo d'Asti

RICOTTA FILLING Combine all ingredients in a medium bowl and mix well.

BREADCRUMB GREMOLATA In a food processor, combine all ingredients and pulse 4–5 times, until a loose crumble has formed.

ASSEMBLY Preheat oven to 450°F. Grease a large baking dish with oil.

Place pasta and sauce into the prepared dish and mix. Dot dollops of ricotta over pasta, then sprinkle with gremolata. Bake for 15 minutes, until the edges are bubbling and the top is golden brown.

Sprinkle with Parmesan, chili flakes, and basil. Drizzle with oil. Season with pepper. Serve with garlic bread.

SERVES **4** / PREP: **15** MINUTES + **30** MINUTES CHILLING TIME / COOK TIME: **10** MINUTES

PAD KRA PAO

I had the pleasure of tasting this dish while staging at a pop-up for Gaggan Anand in San Francisco. When he asked his chef de cuisine to prepare an authentic version, Gaggan couldn't help but smirk. It didn't take long to see why — it was insanely spicy, the kind of spicy that hits you like a freight train. I enjoy spicy food, but this was a 20/10 on the heat scale. Before long, I found myself wearing the same mischievous grin as I served up Pad Kra Pao, fully understanding its fiery charm. Quick and easy, this is a great go-to dish when you are in a hurry. Have everything ready to go before you start cooking because the wok requires a fast pace. Keep up with the heat or get out of the kitchen.

MARINATED PORK
1 Tbsp fish sauce
2 tsp hoisin sauce
2 tsp oyster sauce
2 tsp dark soy sauce
2 tsp soy sauce
1 tsp white vinegar
Zest and juice of 1 lime
1¼ lbs ground pork

PAD KRA PAO
1 Tbsp canola oil
Marinated Pork (see here)
5 red bird's eye chilies
2–3 shallots, finely chopped
2 cloves garlic, finely chopped
¼ stalk lemongrass, thinly sliced
Bunch of Thai basil (see Note), leaves only
White pepper, to taste

ASSEMBLY
½ Tbsp canola oil
½ Tbsp sesame oil
4 eggs
Maggi sauce, to taste (optional)
Pad Kra Pao (see here)
Steamed jasmine rice, to serve
Handful of Thai basil, for garnish
2 red bird's eye chilies, thinly sliced, for sprinkling
2 lime wedges
Grilled Brassicas with Roasted Garlic-Lemon Vinaigrette (page 99), to serve (optional)

PAIRING Off-Dry Riesling

MARINATED PORK In a large bowl, combine all ingredients except pork. Add pork, stir, and refrigerate for 30 minutes.

Remove pork from marinade.

PAD KRA PAO Heat oil in a wok over high heat until it starts to smoke. Swirl oil around to coat the sides of the pan. Add marinated pork and sauté for 4–5 minutes, until browned. (The key is to ensure the pork is not overcrowded and thus maintain a dry stir-fry texture.)

Add chilies, shallots, garlic, lemongrass, and Thai basil. Stir-fry until the ingredients are slightly charred but still firm. Season with white pepper.

ASSEMBLY Heat both oils in a large skillet over high heat. Crack eggs into the pan and fry at high heat. Baste with hot oil until whites are opaque, edges are crispy, and yolks are runny. For extra umami, add 1–2 drops of Maggi sauce to each egg (if using).

Serve stir-fried pork over a bed of warm jasmine rice. Top each plate with a fried egg, Thai basil, a sprinkle of chilies, and a squeeze of lime. If desired, serve with grilled brassicas.

NOTE Thai basil is an herb with a distinct sweet, anise-like flavor, often used in Southeast Asian cuisine. It has a slightly spicy and aromatic taste, which makes it a key ingredient in dishes like Thai green curry, stir-fries, and salads. Thai basil can be found at Asian grocery stores, specialty markets, and larger supermarkets.

BRAISED SPICY PORK HOCKS

I met Haocun Alan Fang, now our chef de cuisine, shortly after opening Aiāna. In those early days, I was young and full of ideas and emotions, and everything felt uncertain and chaotic. I often found myself tangled in the weeds of service or fixated on small mistakes, like missing garnishes. But Alan's calm demeanor and thoughtful nature became a steadying force for the team — me included — helping us navigate the chaos and evolve into the strong, cohesive team we are today at Aiāna. Alan is a man of few words and keeps everything, much like this recipe, simple, short, and sweet. (His favorite expression is, "Why so serious?") Braised with soy sauce, chilies, and pungent spices, this ham hock is so tender and succulent, it practically melts in your mouth. Serve it over steamed rice to soak up the flavorful braising liquid or alongside stir-fried vegetables for a satisfying, hearty meal.

INGREDIENTS

10 dried long bird's eye chilies
2 pork hocks
2 jalapeños
1 orange, quartered
4 cups chicken stock
½ cup Shaoxing wine
2 Tbsp Pixan broad bean paste (see Note)
2 Tbsp soy sauce
2 Tbsp rock sugar
2 tsp dark soy sauce
1 tsp Chinese 13-spice powder (see Note)
Cooked rice, to serve

PAIRING Coors Light (Alan's favorite beer)

Combine all ingredients in a large saucepan or stockpot. Bring to a boil, then reduce heat to medium-low. Cover and simmer for 1½ hours. Remove the lid and cook for another 30 minutes, basting occasionally, until pork is meltingly tender. Transfer pork to a plate.

Increase heat to high and bring the braising liquid to a boil. Boil for 8–12 minutes, until reduced by half. Add pork back to the pan and stir to coat in the glaze.

Serve hot with rice.

NOTES Pixan broad bean paste is a rich, umami-packed fermented paste made from broad beans, salt, and spices, commonly used in Southeast Asian and Chinese cuisines to add depth and savory complexity to dishes like stir-fries, sauces, and braises.

Chinese 13-spice powder is a fragrant blend of spices that includes star anise, cinnamon, Sichuan peppercorns, and other warming ingredients, perfect for adding a bold, complex flavor to meats, stews, and dumplings.

Both are available at well-stocked Asian supermarkets or can be purchased online.

SERVES 4 / PREP: 10 MINUTES + 25 MINUTES STANDING TIME / COOK TIME: 15 MINUTES + 1 HOUR SOUS VIDE

MONTREAL-SPICED STEAK

Montreal steak is a seasoning blend inspired by the bold, smoky flavors of Montreal's Jewish delis, originally adapted from the spices used for smoked meats. Typically made with garlic, black pepper, and coriander, it's a popular rub for grilled meats. This is my favorite way to prepare a steak, whether at home or in a restaurant. It has incredible flavor and melts in your mouth. The best part? You can prep everything ahead of time.

SOUS VIDE STEAK

5 Tbsp melted butter
4 (12-oz) aged New York strip steaks
3 cloves garlic
5 sprigs thyme
Sprig of rosemary
Sprig of sage

SPICE BLEND

1 Tbsp onion flakes
1 Tbsp granulated garlic
1 Tbsp coriander seeds
1 Tbsp dill seeds
1 tsp chili flakes
¼ tsp cayenne powder
½ tsp yellow mustard powder
1 Tbsp salt
1 Tbsp black pepper

ASSEMBLY

Sous Vide Steak (see here)
Salt and black pepper, to taste
Spice Blend (see here)
¼ cup tallow (divided)
5 sprigs thyme
3 cloves garlic
2 Tbsp honey butter
Chimichurri (page 166), to serve (optional)

PAIRING California Cabernet Sauvignon

SOUS VIDE STEAK Cook butter in a small saucepan over medium heat and stir for 6–8 minutes, until golden brown. (This is your brown butter.)

Combine the remaining ingredients in a vacuum-sealed bag. Add 3 tablespoons of brown butter. Sous vide at 120°F for 1 hour.

Transfer the bag of steaks to a large bowl of ice water to stop cooking and help gelatinize the juices. Remove steaks from the bag, then dry them thoroughly on a wire rack lined with paper towels.

SPICE BLEND Combine all ingredients in a small bowl and mix well.

ASSEMBLY Pat steaks completely dry, discarding thyme, rosemary, and sage. Season steaks with salt and pepper. Press the fat cap of each steak into spice blend, distributing it evenly. Set aside for 18 minutes.

Heat a large cast-iron skillet over medium-high heat until it begins to smoke. Add 1 tablespoon of tallow and let it melt completely. Carefully lay steaks in the pan, positioning them away from you to prevent splattering, and sear for 2 minutes on each side. Press down lightly with your fingers or use a meat weight for an even sear. This process develops the rich crust and deep flavor, but excessively high heat can scorch the steak instead of enhancing its flavor.

Add the remaining ingredients. Baste steaks for 1½ minutes on each side. Transfer steaks to a cutting board, tent with aluminum foil, and set aside for 6 minutes. Discard thyme. Slice into 1-inch pieces.

Serve with chimichurri (if using).

SERVES **4** / PREP: **20** MINUTES + **30** MINUTES RESTING TIME / COOK TIME: ~**1½** HOURS

CARIBBEAN CURRY BEEF

It's curry beef, not beef curry! Wrapped in a buttery, flaky roti or served over steamed rice, this dish is one of my all-time favorites. Every household or roti shop has its own twist, and this is my version. Feel free to personalize it. Add your own creative take on things, and make a curry that's uniquely yours!

INGREDIENTS

1 (16-oz) beef chuck, cut into 1½-inch cubes
2 Scotch bonnet chilies, seeded and finely chopped
2 tsp salt, plus extra to taste
1 tsp black pepper, plus extra to taste
3 Tbsp coconut oil
3 bay leaves
½ cup Red Stripe Beer
3 cups beef stock
1 cup coconut cream
2 Tbsp Jamaican curry powder
10 sprigs thyme
1 small onion, chopped
1 potato, cut into ½-inch cubes
1 small red bell pepper, seeded, deveined, and chopped
½ sweet potato, cut into cubes
4–5 cloves garlic, finely chopped
1½ Tbsp finely grated ginger
1 tsp lime juice
¼ cup cilantro, for garnish
Steamed rice or roti, to serve
Lime wedges, to serve

PAIRING Argentinian Malbec

In a large bowl, combine beef, chilies, salt, and pepper. Set aside to rest for 30 minutes.

Heat oil in a Dutch oven over medium heat. Add bay leaves and cook for 1–2 minutes, until fragrant. Working in batches, sear beef until browned. Transfer to a plate.

Pour in beer and deglaze, scraping the bottom of the pan to release any browned bits.

In a medium bowl, combine stock, coconut cream, and curry powder. Add the mixture to the pan and bring to a boil. Reduce heat to medium-low and simmer. Add beef and thyme. Cover and simmer for 1 hour, until meat is fork tender.

Skim any excess fat from the surface of the curry. Stir in vegetables, garlic, and ginger. Cover and simmer for another 30 minutes, until vegetables are tender and the sauce has reduced. If the sauce needs thickening, remove some sweet potato from the pot. Mash it with a fork in a small bowl, then stir it back in. (The starch will thicken the curry.) Discard bay leaves and thyme. Season to taste with salt and pepper. Pour in lime juice.

Garnish with cilantro and serve with rice (or roti) and lime wedges.

SERVES **4** / PREP: **20** MINUTES / COOK TIME: **2 ½** HOURS

FIRE-ROASTED LAMB BIRRIA TACOS

Here is a combination of two of my favorite foods, tacos and lamb birria. Lamb birria is a rich, soul-warming Mexican stew where tender, slow-cooked lamb absorbs a complex medley of smoky, spicy chilies and savory seasonings. Leftover birria can also be transformed into a "flacho," a genius creation by my buddy and nacho master Josh Evraire. It's a single layer of nachos with each chip carefully topped to cater to the unique tastes of every guest.

INGREDIENTS

6 dried chipotle peppers
4 Anaheim chilies
4 guajillo chilies
¼ cup white vinegar
2 cups water
6 Tbsp canola oil (divided)
2 lamb shanks
Salt and black pepper, to taste
4 cloves garlic
3 jalapeños + 1 finely chopped jalapeño (divided)
½ onion
1 large tomato, chopped (1 cup)
½ cup cilantro stems
3 bay leaves
1 Mexican cinnamon stick (see Note)
2 Tbsp cumin seeds
2 Tbsp coriander seeds
2 Tbsp paprika
2 Tbsp dried Mexican oregano (see Note)
1 Tbsp Tajín
8 cups lamb stock or water
1 cup chopped cilantro (divided)
Lime juice
12 tortillas
Grated cheese, such as Oaxaca, mozzarella, Monterey Jack, cheddar
Finely chopped Spanish onion
Arroz Rojo (page 76), to serve
Traditional garnishes, such as jalapeños, chilies, red onions, radishes, salsa, sour cream, to serve
Lime wedges, to serve

PAIRING Chianti Classico

In a small saucepan, combine chipotle peppers, Anaheim chilies, guajillo chilies, vinegar, and water. Bring to a boil and simmer for 15 minutes. Set aside to cool slightly.

Transfer the mixture to a blender and purée until smooth. Set aside.

Preheat a grill to high heat.

Brush 1 tablespoon of oil over lamb, then season with salt and pepper. Add lamb to the grill and char all over for 6–8 minutes. (This seals the meat to lock in moisture while braising and imparts a smokiness authentic to a Mexican cooking style.) Set aside.

In a Dutch oven or large skillet, combine garlic, 3 jalapeños, onion, tomato, and cilantro stems and dry-roast over high heat until blackened. Try to keep vegetables as whole as possible. Transfer to a large bowl and cover immediately with plastic wrap. Set aside for 5 minutes.

Peel off the outer charred skin from vegetables, then combine them in a food processor and blend until smooth. Set aside.

Heat the remaining 5 tablespoons of oil in the same Dutch oven over medium-high heat. Add bay leaves, cinnamon, cumin seeds, and coriander seeds and heat for 1 minute, until fragrant. Add puréed vegetables, paprika, oregano, and Tajín. Sauté for 30 seconds to cook off the spices.

Add the pepper mixture and lamb and pour in stock (or water). Season with salt and pepper. Cover and simmer over medium heat for 1¾ hours, until lamb is tender and practically falls off the bone. (Yeah, you know it's going to be good!) Transfer lamb to a plate.

Strain the cooking liquid into a large saucepan. Discard the solids. Shred lamb and reserve in the cooking liquid. Bring to a boil, then season with ½ cup of cilantro and lime juice. Skim fat, reserving it in a medium bowl. The remaining cooking liquid will be the dipping jus for the taco, which can also be enjoyed as a soup!

Heat a large nonstick skillet over low heat. Dip 4 tortillas into the birria fat and place them in the pan. Add a bit of cheese and meat. Cook the tacos open face until cheese begins to melt. Top with more cilantro, onion, and chopped jalapeño. Using a spatula, fold the tacos in half and cook for another 2 minutes, until cheese is melted and tortillas are crispy. The tacos should maintain their shape and not be pliable!

Serve with dipping jus, arroz rojo, traditional garnishes, and lime wedges.

NOTES Mexican cinnamon, also known as *canela*, is softer, sweeter, and more fragrant than regular cinnamon, with a delicate, almost citrusy flavor and a finer texture. Mexican cinnamon is key to achieving that authentic, rich depth in Mexican and Latin American recipes, but you can use regular cinnamon if needed.

Mexican oregano is more robust, citrusy, and peppery, with earthy notes, making it perfect for bold Latin American dishes, while Mediterranean oregano is milder, sweeter, and better suited for Italian and Mediterranean recipes.

6

drinks + desserts

MANGO AND CARDAMOM LASSI

This mango and cardamom lassi is sunshine in a glass! It's the kind of drink that cools you down and awakens your taste buds with every sip.

INGREDIENTS

1½ cups milk
1 cup diced fresh mango
1 cup sugar
½ tsp ground cardamom
1 tsp vanilla extract
Honey, to rim glasses (optional)
Tajín, to rim glasses (optional)
1½ cups puréed mango
1 cup Greek yogurt
4 sprigs mint, for garnish (optional)
4 slices dried mango, for garnish (optional)
1 cup whipped cream, for garnish
Saffron threads, for garnish

Warm milk in a small saucepan to 98°F. Whisk in fresh mango, sugar, cardamom, and vanilla until well combined. Remove from heat and steep for 3-5 minutes to infuse the flavors. Strain the mixture through a fine-mesh sieve to remove any solids, then refrigerate for 50 minutes, until cold.

Meanwhile, rim four glasses with honey and Tajín, if desired. Place glasses and a high-powered blender jug in the fridge for 10 minutes to chill.

Pour the milk mixture into the cold blender. Add puréed mango and yogurt. Blend on high speed until smooth, creamy, and frothy.

Pour the lassi over ice into chilled glasses. Garnish each with mint and dried mango (if using), then top with whipped cream and saffron threads. Serve immediately.

CHOCOLATE AND HAZELNUT MILKSHAKE

Fun fact: Milkshakes began in the late nineteenth century as a rich, whiskey-infused drink made with milk and eggs—and no ice cream. It wasn't until the 1920s that ice cream was added, and the electric blender transformed them into the creamy, sweet indulgence that became a soda fountain classic. This chocolate and hazelnut milkshake is a nod to the original milkshake: a grown-up indulgence combining caramelized hazelnuts, rich dark chocolate, a praline-crusted rim, and a luscious chocolate drizzle. The ice cream is served on top for the perfect balance of texture and richness.

INGREDIENTS

½ cup hazelnuts
¼ cup sugar
4 oz dark chocolate
¼ cup chocolate hazelnut spread, plus extra for coating
2 cups chocolate milk
4 scoops chocolate ice cream
1 cup whipped cream
4 wafer straws
¼ cup chocolate shavings

Chill a blender jug and 4 mugs in the fridge for 10 minutes. Line a baking sheet with greased parchment paper.

Toast hazelnuts in a small skillet over medium heat until golden brown. Sprinkle sugar into the pan and stir continuously until golden and caramelized. Remove from heat.

Spread caramelized hazelnuts onto the prepared baking sheet. Set aside to cool completely. Using a mortar and pestle or food processor, crush into small pieces.

Melt dark chocolate in a small saucepan over low heat, stirring frequently to prevent sticking. Set aside.

To the chilled blender, add melted chocolate, reserving some for drizzling; 1 tablespoon of hazelnut praline; chocolate hazelnut spread; and chocolate milk. Blend until smooth and frothy, ensuring the melted chocolate is broken down into fine bits.

Drizzle reserved melted chocolate along the insides of the chilled mugs. Coat the rim of each with chocolate hazelnut spread, then press the remaining crushed hazelnut praline onto the coated rim.

Fill mugs with ice cubes, then pour in the milkshake. Top each milkshake with chocolate ice cream, whipped cream, a wafer straw, and chocolate shavings. Serve immediately.

CONNOR'S MEZCAL SOUR

Our bartender Connor Clune first discovered this drink in a Montreal bar, and since then, it's become his signature. A master at improvisation, he's known for crafting custom cocktails that hit every note of a guest's unique taste. He calls each cocktail "the dealer's choice" — because when Connor's behind the bar, you always have a winning hand.

INGREDIENTS
1¼ fl oz mezcal
½ fl oz dry curaçao
½ fl oz limoncello
1 fl oz lemon juice
1 egg white

Combine all ingredients in a cocktail mixer and dry shake for 5 seconds. Add ice and shake for 5 seconds.

Strain into a low-ball glass with ice cubes.

MAKES **20** / PREP: **15** MINUTES + **1** HOUR CHILLING TIME / COOK TIME: **10–15** MINUTES

MATCHA AND RED BEAN MADELEINES

Bold matcha and subtly sweet red bean paste come together in a truly exceptional flavor pairing. With crisp edges and a tender crumb, these treats offer elegance with a delightful twist. Serve with tea or coffee and prepare to impress. Your dessert game just leveled up.

INGREDIENTS

1 cup sugar
2 Tbsp red bean paste
1 Tbsp honey
1 tsp molasses
4 eggs
1½ cups all-purpose flour
1 Tbsp matcha powder
¾ tsp baking powder
Pinch of salt
⅔ cup (1⅓ sticks) butter, melted and cooled
1 tsp almond extract
Nonstick cooking spray
Icing sugar, for dusting

PAIRING Hokkaido latte

In a large bowl, combine granulated sugar, red bean paste, honey, molasses, and eggs and mix until smooth.

In a medium bowl, sift together flour, matcha powder, baking powder, and salt. Gradually add the dry ingredients to the egg mixture and stir until combined. Pour in melted butter and almond extract and mix until the batter is smooth and glossy. Transfer the batter to a piping bag and chill in the fridge for 1 hour.

Preheat oven to 375°F. Grease madeleine molds with nonstick cooking spray.

Pipe the batter into the prepared molds, filling each cavity about two-thirds full. Bake for 10–12 minutes, until the edges are golden brown and the centers spring back when lightly touched. Remove from the oven, then set aside to cool for 5 minutes. Gently release the madeleines onto a wire rack.

Dust with icing sugar and serve.

CHOCOLATE CHIP COOKIES

Chocolate chip cookies are iconic, but this recipe elevates them to a whole new level. Subtle hints of molasses, a touch of coffee, and a whisper of nutmeg add unexpected depth, resulting in cookies that are unapologetically indulgent — just as they should be. This is genuinely the best cookie I've ever had.

INGREDIENTS

½ cup milk chocolate chunks
1¼ cups + 1 tsp all-purpose flour (divided)
½ cup (1 stick) very soft butter
½ cup sugar
¾ cup brown sugar
1 egg
1 egg yolk
1 tsp molasses
1 tsp instant coffee powder
Dash of ground nutmeg
½ tsp baking soda
1 tsp salt
1 cup dark chocolate chips, plus extra for topping
Flaky sea salt, for sprinkling

PAIRING Cold milk or strong Americano

In a small bowl, combine chocolate chunks with 1 teaspoon of flour. (This helps prevent the chunks from sinking to the bottom of the cookies and ensures an even distribution of chocolate throughout.)

In a stand mixer fitted with a paddle attachment, cream butter and both sugars until light and fluffy, scraping down the sides of the bowl as needed. Add egg and egg yolk and mix until fully combined. Mix in molasses, instant coffee, and nutmeg until thoroughly combined.

In a medium bowl, sift together the remaining 1¼ cups of flour, baking soda, and salt. Gradually add the dry ingredients to the butter mixture, mixing just until combined. Do not overmix. Fold in chocolate chips and prepared chocolate chunks. Remove the dough from the mixer, wrap it in plastic wrap, and chill in the fridge for 15 minutes.

Preheat oven to 350°F. Line a baking sheet with parchment paper.

Roll the chilled dough into 8 equal portions and place them on the prepared baking sheet, evenly spaced 2 inches apart. Press a few extra chocolate chips on top of each ball. Bake for 8–12 minutes, until the edges are golden and the centers are just set. Set aside on a wire rack until slightly cooled.

Serve warm with a pinch of flaky sea salt.

MAKES **8** / PREP: **20** MINUTES + **15** MINUTES CHILLING TIME / COOK TIME: **10–15** MINUTES

CHAI SNICKER-DOODLES

A cozy spin on a classic cookie! The warm spices of chai infuse these snickerdoodles with a rich, utterly irresistible depth of flavor. They're soft, chewy, and perfectly sweet — just the right treat for sipping alongside tea or coffee. We love baking these on chilly winter nights, turning a snow day into something truly special.

CHAI SPICE
3 Tbsp ground cinnamon
1 Tbsp ground cardamom
1 Tbsp ground ginger
½ Tbsp ground nutmeg
½ Tbsp ground cloves
1 tsp mace

DOUGH
½ cup (1 stick) butter, softened
⅔ cup sugar
1 egg
1 egg yolk
1¼ cups all-purpose flour
1½ tsp Chai Spice (see here)
1 tsp cream of tartar
½ tsp salt
½ tsp baking soda

COATING
½ cup sugar
4 tsp Chai Spice (see here)

PAIRING Hot toddy

CHAI SPICE Combine all ingredients in a small bowl.

DOUGH In a stand mixer fitted with a paddle attachment, cream butter and sugar until light and fluffy, scraping down the sides of the bowl as needed. Add egg and egg yolk and mix until fully combined.

In a medium bowl, sift together flour, chai spice, cream of tartar, salt, and baking soda. Gradually add the dry ingredients to the butter mixture and mix until just combined. Do not overmix. Remove the dough from the bowl, wrap it in plastic wrap, and refrigerate for 15 minutes.

COATING Combine both ingredients in a small bowl.

ASSEMBLY Preheat oven to 350°F. Line a baking sheet with parchment paper.

Remove the dough from the fridge and divide into 8 equal portions. Roll each into a ball, then cover evenly with coating. Place the coated dough balls on the prepared baking sheet, evenly spaced apart. Bake for 8-12 minutes, until the edges are just set and the centers are slightly soft. Transfer cookies to a wire rack to cool slightly.

Serve warm.

SERVES **4** / PREP: **15** MINUTES / COOK TIME: ~**3 ¼** HOURS

DULCE DE LECHE CHURROS

Churros are pure indulgence, but the dulce de leche takes this recipe to new heights. The caramel adds a decadent richness that pairs beautifully with the spiced sugar coating. Whether dipped or devoured straight, these churros deliver on comfort.

DULCE DE LECHE SAUCE
1 (10-oz/300-mL) can sweetened condensed milk

CHURROS
½ cup milk
3 Tbsp butter
2 tsp sugar
½ tsp salt
⅔ cup all-purpose flour, sifted
2 eggs
1 tsp vanilla extract
3 cups canola oil, for frying

CINNAMON SUGAR
1 cup sugar
1 Tbsp Mexican cinnamon (see Note)
1 tsp ground nutmeg

ASSEMBLY
Churros (see here)
Cinnamon Sugar (see here)
Dulce de Leche Sauce (see here), to serve

PAIRING Mexican hot chocolate

DULCE DE LECHE SAUCE Place the can of sweetened condensed milk in a medium saucepan of water. Simmer over medium-low heat for 3 hours, ensuring that the can is always submerged. (You can top it with a plate or meat weight.)

CHURROS In a small saucepan, combine milk, butter, sugar, and salt. Bring to a rapid simmer over medium heat. Reduce heat to medium-low, then add flour and stir until a paste forms and a skin develops on the bottom of the pot. Remove from heat and set aside to cool.

Add eggs one at a time, mixing well after each addition. Continue mixing until a smooth paste forms. Stir in vanilla. Transfer the churro paste to a piping bag fitted with an open star tip.

Pour oil into a deep fryer or deep saucepan and heat to a temperature of 350°F. Carefully pipe churros into the pan, taking care not to splash hot oil. Use scissors to cut the dough at the desired length. Work in batches to avoid overcrowding. Deep-fry for 3–4 minutes, until golden brown. Transfer to a paper towel–lined plate.

CINNAMON SUGAR Combine all ingredients in a medium bowl.

ASSEMBLY Roll churros in the cinnamon-sugar mixture until well coated. Serve warm with dulce de leche sauce.

NOTE Mexican cinnamon, or *canela*, stands out for its mild, sweet aroma and soft, easily crumbled texture, offering a distinct contrast to the stronger, more common version. It's available at Latin markets, specialty food stores, and online.

MAKES **24** BITES / PREP: **25** MINUTES + **4** HOURS FREEZING TIME + AT LEAST **1** HOUR CHILLING TIME / COOK TIME: **5** MINUTES

PINEAPPLE AND PEACH CHEESECAKE

Luscious, creamy, and endlessly versatile, cheesecake is the perfect canvas for both classic and adventurous flavors. This no-bake version combines the tropical sweetness of pineapple and peach with the richness of cream cheese to create a dessert that's indulgent yet refreshing. With a hint of cinnamon and a buttery graham cracker crust, these bite-sized treats are easy to make and even easier to devour — perfect for when you want a show-stopping dessert without the fuss.

INGREDIENTS

1½ Tbsp gelatin powder
Generous 1 cup cream cheese, softened
⅓ cup sugar
Pinch of salt
1 tsp vanilla extract
¼ cup diced pineapple
¼ cup diced peaches
¾ cup heavy (35%) cream (divided)
2 cups finely ground graham crackers
½ cup cookie butter (see Note), melted
1 tsp ground cinnamon
Dried pineapple slices, for garnish
Dried peach slices, for garnish

PAIRING Poiré

In a small bowl, combine gelatin powder and 2 tablespoons of water. Set aside to bloom.

In a stand mixer fitted with a paddle attachment, combine cream cheese, sugar, salt, and vanilla. Mix until smooth.

In a small saucepan, combine diced pineapple, diced peaches, and ¼ cup of cream. Cook over medium-low heat, until the fruit is tender. Remove from heat.

Stir in the bloomed gelatin into fruit until gelatin has dissolved. Fold the fruit mixture into the cream cheese mixture. Pour in the remaining ½ cup of cream and mix until smooth. Transfer the mixture to a piping bag.

In a medium bowl, combine ground graham crackers, melted cookie butter, and cinnamon.

Pipe the cream cheese mixture into a 24-cavity silicone mold, filling each cavity three-quarters full. Top with the graham cracker mixture and press lightly to pack. Place mold in the freezer and freeze for 4 hours, until set.

Remove the cheesecake bites from the mold, then refrigerate for at least 1 hour.

Garnish with dried pineapple and peaches and serve cold.

NOTE Cookie butter is a sweet, spiced spread made from crushed speculoos cookies, offering a rich and caramelized flavor with hints of cinnamon and other spices. You can typically find it at specialty food stores, larger supermarkets, or online.

JAPANESE-STYLE FRUIT SANDWICH

This fruit sandwich transforms simple ingredients into a work of edible art. Fluffy milk bread cradles luscious Chantilly cream and vibrant slices of fresh fruit, creating a treat that is as visually stunning as it is delicious. Perfectly chilled and bursting with juicy, sweet flavors, it's a dessert that feels indulgent yet refreshingly light.

INGREDIENTS

1¼ cups heavy (35%) cream
¼ cup icing sugar, sifted
1 vanilla bean, seeds scraped
Zest of 1 lemon
8 slices Milk Bread (page 57), crusts removed
4 strawberries, halved
8 cotton candy grapes, trimmed
2 kiwis, sliced
1 mango, sliced
1 peach, sliced

PAIRING Sparkling peach cider

In a stand mixer fitted with a whisk attachment, combine cream, icing sugar, vanilla seeds, and lemon zest and whisk until stiff peaks form. Transfer Chantilly cream to a piping bag fitted with a ¼-inch circular tip.

Arrange the slices of milk bread in pairs, matching the top and bottom slices for each sandwich. Pipe a layer of Chantilly cream onto the bottom slice of each pair, then arrange fruit on top, creating a vibrant, symmetrical display that will be revealed when sliced. Pipe another layer of cream over the fruit, then gently press the top slice of bread onto the cream.

Wrap each sandwich tightly in plastic wrap and refrigerate for at least 1 hour but ideally overnight for optimal results.

Before unwrapping, slice sandwiches into rectangles to reveal the vibrant fruit arrangement. Unwrap, then trim the edges with a sharp knife for clean lines, if desired. Serve chilled.

SERVES **4** / PREP: **20** MINUTES + AT LEAST **24** HOURS CHILLING TIME + **2** HOURS FREEZING TIME / COOK TIME: **20** MINUTES

VANILLA ICE CREAM

Vanilla ice cream is a versatile base that invites creativity, serving as the perfect starting point for endless customizations. Whether you fold in swirls of chocolate, fresh berry compote, or crushed cookies, or infuse the base with unique flavors like Earl Grey tea or espresso, this recipe is your gateway to crafting ice cream that is as adventurous or comforting as you like. For added texture, feel free to fold in chunks of cookies, caramel swirls, or nuts at the end of churning. A personal favorite is combining Kinder Bueno pieces with cheesecake chunks (page 154) and a drizzle of dulce de leche (page 153).

INGREDIENTS

4 egg yolks
¾ cup sugar
Pinch of salt
2 cups heavy (35%) cream
1 cup milk
1 vanilla bean, seeds scraped

PAIRING A shot of espresso

Bring water to a boil in a medium saucepan.

Combine all ingredients in a medium heatproof bowl. Place the bowl over the boiling water, ensuring the bottom doesn't touch the water, and whisk constantly. Remove from heat periodically, scraping down the sides of the bowl to prevent the mixture from sticking. Return to the heat and whisk until custard is thick enough to coat the back of a spoon. Take care not to overheat the mixture; otherwise, it will curdle. (If curdling occurs, you'll need to start over.)

Place the bowl of custard over a bowl of ice water, whisking constantly to release steam. Once cooled, refrigerate for at least 24 hours.

Prepare your ice-cream machine by pre-freezing all necessary components. Pour the chilled custard into the machine and churn according to the manufacturer's instructions, checking frequently to ensure smooth operation.

Transfer ice cream to an airtight container and freeze for at least 2 hours to firm up. Serve.

MAPLE TAFFY

I'll never forget the time I was traveling through the heart of Quebec and stumbled upon a little shack where an elderly man was stirring a bubbling cauldron of taffy over an open flame. The scent hit me like a wave. It truly is liquid gold! This Canadian classic is pure maple magic. Warm, gooey taffy poured over snow (or ice) transforms into a chewy, sweet treat that melts in your mouth. It's a simple, nostalgic dessert that's sure to bring a smile every time.

INGREDIENTS
2 cups authentic maple syrup
Shaved ice or snow (see Note)
Flaky sea salt

SPECIAL EQUIPMENT
Popsicle sticks

PAIRING Canadian rye

In a small saucepan, bring maple syrup to a boil and using a candy thermometer, heat to 239°F. Maintain this temperature for 2 minutes.

Spread snow onto a baking sheet. Create shallow indents in snow to form molds for the taffy. Cool hot maple syrup to 220°F, then carefully pour it into the prepared indents.

Sprinkle the taffy with a pinch of sea salt for a perfect balance of sweetness and savoriness. Let the taffy set for 5-10 seconds, just long enough to firm up slightly.

Using a popsicle stick, roll the taffy into a neat spiral. Serve directly into the hands of your guests for a nostalgic treat with a salty twist.

NOTE You can crush ice into a snow-like texture using a snow cone machine or gather fresh, clean snow if available.

7
basics

From sweet treats and creamy aiolis to pickled vegetables and versatile dressings, these recipes serve as the backbone for culinary creativity. Perfect as stand-alone components or complementary additions to a dish, each recipe is crafted to deliver flavors.

MAKES **1** CUP
PREP: **10** MINUTES / COOK TIME: **30** MINUTES

Roasted Garlic-Lemon Vinaigrette

INGREDIENTS

4 cloves garlic
2 lemons, halved
¼ small shallot
Extra-virgin olive oil for drizzling
1 Tbsp Dijon mustard
1 Tbsp finely chopped parsley
1 Tbsp finely chopped chives
2 tsp red wine vinegar
1 tsp chili flakes
Zest of 1 lemon
Salt and black pepper, to taste
½ cup extra-virgin olive oil

Preheat oven to 375°F. Line a baking sheet with a piece of aluminum foil.

Combine garlic, lemon halves, and shallot on the prepared baking sheet. Drizzle with oil and roast for 30 minutes. Set aside. When cool enough to handle, use a fork to remove the juice from the lemon. Discard seeds and rinds.

In a blender, combine all ingredients except the ½ cup of oil and blend until smooth. With the motor still running, gradually add oil and blend until emulsified.

The vinaigrette can be stored in an airtight container for 5 days in the fridge.

MAKES ABOUT **2** CUPS
PREP: **10** MINUTES

Chimichurri

INGREDIENTS
2–3 jalapeños, finely chopped (½ cup)
1 small red onion, finely chopped (½ cup)
1 small clove garlic, finely chopped
1 Tbsp finely chopped parsley
2 tsp finely chopped cilantro
1 tsp finely chopped mint
1 tsp salt
½ tsp black pepper
¼ tsp chili flakes
¼ cup extra-virgin olive oil
¼ cup red wine vinegar
Zest and juice of 1 lime

Combine all ingredients in a medium bowl, then set aside for 30 minutes. Serve at room temperature.

The chimichurri can be stored in an airtight container for 1 week in the fridge.

MAKES **1** CUP
PREP: **5** MINUTES / COOK TIME: **5** MINUTES

Yuzu Ponzu

INGREDIENTS
2 (3-inch) pieces kombu seaweed
1 cup premium soy sauce
¼ cup mirin
1 Tbsp bonito
¼ cup yuzu juice

Combine all ingredients except yuzu juice in a small saucepan and bring to a boil. Reduce heat to medium-low and simmer for 2 minutes. Strain.

Stir in yuzu juice, then set aside to cool.

The ponzu can be stored in an airtight container for 1 month in the fridge.

MAKES 1 CUP
PREP: 10 MINUTES + 10 MINUTES STANDING TIME

Sumac Tzatziki

This tzatziki pairs beautifully with grilled meats and roasted vegetables or is a refreshing dip for flatbreads.

INGREDIENTS

½ small cucumber, peeled and grated (1 cup)
Salt, to taste
3 cloves garlic, grated
1 Tbsp finely chopped red onions
1 cup Greek yogurt
2 tsp finely chopped mint
2 tsp lemon juice
2 tsp finely chopped dill
2 tsp sumac
1 tsp lime juice
1 tsp extra-virgin olive oil
Black pepper, to taste

Place cucumber in a small bowl and sprinkle with salt. Set aside for 10 minutes to draw out excess moisture. Transfer cucumber to a cheesecloth or fine-mesh strainer and squeeze to remove as much liquid as possible.

In a separate small bowl, combine cucumber, garlic, and onions. Add the remaining ingredients and whisk until well combined. Chill.

The tzatziki can be stored in an airtight container for 3 days in the fridge.

MAKES **2** CUPS
PREP: **10** MINUTES

Cantina Guacamole

INGREDIENTS
3 ripe avocados
1 clove garlic, finely chopped
Zest and juice of 1 lime
1 Tbsp finely chopped red onions
1 Tbsp finely chopped scallions
1 Tbsp finely chopped tomatoes
2 tsp finely chopped cilantro
1 tsp finely chopped jalapeños
¼ tsp ground cumin
¼ tsp ground coriander
Salt and black pepper, to taste

In a medium bowl, combine all ingredients. Using a fork, mash avocados to your desired consistency.

The guacamole can be stored in an airtight container for 2 days in the fridge.

MAKES ¾ CUP
PREP: **10** MINUTES

Old Bay Remoulade

INGREDIENTS
1 clove garlic, finely chopped
1 Tbsp chopped scallions
1 Tbsp chopped chives
2 tsp finely chopped shallots
2 tsp finely chopped celery
2 tsp Old Bay seasoning
Black pepper, to taste
½ cup mayonnaise
2 tsp Dijon mustard
2 tsp lemon juice
1 tsp Tapatío (see Note on page 76)
Zest of 1 lemon

Mix all ingredients in a small bowl until combined.

The remoulade can be stored in an airtight container for 5 days in the fridge.

MAKES **3½** CUPS
PREP: **10** MINUTES

Mint Raita

INGREDIENTS

3 cups Greek yogurt
¼ cup grated cucumber, strained of excess moisture
1 Tbsp finely chopped red onions
1 Tbsp finely chopped tomatoes
1 Tbsp finely chopped cilantro, plus extra for garnish
1 Tbsp thinly sliced mint
Zest of 1 lime
2 tsp lime juice
Salt and black pepper, to taste
1 tsp toasted ground cumin, for sprinkling

Combine all ingredients except ground cumin in a medium bowl and mix well. Sprinkle with ground cumin and garnish with cilantro. Serve chilled.

The raita can be stored in an airtight container for 2 days in the fridge.

MAKES **1** CUP
PREP: **10** MINUTES

Ramp Ranch

The quantity of wild garlic, or ramps, in this recipe may seem small, but the bold, raw flavor makes a significant impact. Adding more could cause the dressing to become too sharp, almost like raw garlic. This careful balance allows the ramps to impart their unique taste without overpowering the dish.

INGREDIENTS

½ cup mayonnaise
½ cup sour cream
2 Tbsp buttermilk
2 tsp garlic powder
2 tsp onion powder
2 tsp finely chopped wild garlic (ramps)
1 tsp finely chopped chives
1 tsp finely chopped parsley
1 tsp finely chopped dill
1 tsp salt
1 tsp black pepper

Combine all ingredients in a small bowl. Whisk until smooth.

The dipping sauce can be stored in an airtight container for 5 days in the fridge.

MAYONNAISES AND AIOLIS

MAKES ¾ CUP
PREP: **5** MINUTES

Dijonnaise

INGREDIENTS

½ cup mayonnaise
1 Tbsp grainy mustard
2 tsp Dijon mustard
1 tsp horseradish
1 tsp lemon juice
1 tsp salt
1 tsp black pepper

Combine all ingredients in a small bowl and whisk until smooth. Transfer to a squeeze bottle for use.

The Dijonnaise can be stored in an airtight container for 1 month in the fridge.

MAKES **1¼** CUPS
PREP: **10** MINUTES

Chili Mayo

INGREDIENTS
1 cup mayonnaise
2 Tbsp chili oil
1 tsp finely chopped cilantro
½ tsp lime zest
1 tsp lime juice
½ tsp white pepper
½ tsp black pepper
Salt, to taste

Combine all ingredients in a small bowl and whisk until smooth.

The mayo can be stored in an airtight container for 7 days in the fridge.

MAKES **1** CUP
PREP: **10** MINUTES

Sesame Kewpie

INGREDIENTS
1 cup Kewpie mayonnaise
2 tsp toasted sesame seeds
2 tsp tahini
1 tsp sesame oil
1 tsp finely grated ginger
1 tsp finely grated garlic
Zest of 1 lime

Combine all ingredients in a small bowl and whisk until smooth.

The Kewpie mayonnaise can be stored in an airtight container for 7 days in the fridge.

MAKES **1** CUP
PREP: **15** MINUTES / COOK TIME: **5** MINUTES

Parsley Aioli

INGREDIENTS

1 Tbsp + 1 tsp salt (divided)
Bunch of parsley
2 egg yolks
1 Tbsp mustard
4 tsp apple cider vinegar
Zest of 1 lemon
½ tsp black pepper
1 cup canola oil
2 tsp lemon juice

Bring a large saucepan of water to a boil and add 1 tablespoon of salt. Blanch parsley for 30 seconds. Drain, then transfer to a bowl of ice water. Drain and squeeze out excess moisture.

Finely chop parsley and place in a blender. Add egg yolks, mustard, vinegar, lemon zest, the remaining 1 teaspoon of salt, and pepper. Blend until smooth. With the motor still running on medium speed, gradually add oil and blend until emulsified. Increase speed and finish with lemon juice. Blend until smooth.

The parsley aioli can be stored in an airtight container for 3 days in the fridge.

MAKES **1** CUP
PREP: **10** MINUTES / COOK TIME: **5** MINUTES

Vadouvan Tartar Sauce

Vadouvan is a fragrant French-inspired curry blend that combines traditional Indian spices with fragrant aromatics. It is milder and more nuanced than standard curry powder, with a hint of smokiness and caramelized onion sweetness. You can find it at specialty spice shops, gourmet grocery stores, or online.

INGREDIENTS

2 tsp butter
2 tsp vadouvan spice powder
1 clove garlic, finely chopped
1 Tbsp finely chopped capers
1 Tbsp finely chopped shallots
1 tsp finely chopped chives
1 tsp finely chopped dill
1 tsp finely chopped parsley
Zest of 1 lemon
1 cup mayonnaise
1 Tbsp lemon juice
1 Tbsp Dijon mustard
2 tsp malt vinegar
Salt and black pepper, to taste

Melt butter in a small saucepan over low heat. Add vadouvan and bloom for 1 minute. Set aside to cool to room temperature.

In a small bowl, combine the seasoned butter and remaining ingredients. Mix well.

PICKLES AND PICKLING LIQUID

MAKES **1** GALLON
PREP: **10** MINUTES / COOK TIME: **10** MINUTES

Pickling Liquid

INGREDIENTS
30 black peppercorns
6 cloves garlic
6 whole cloves
4 bay leaves
4 star anise
2 cinnamon sticks
2 cups sugar
2 cups salt
2 Tbsp coriander seeds
2 tsp chili flakes
Bunch of dill
4 quarts vinegar

Combine all ingredients in a large stockpot and bring to a boil. Remove from heat, then set aside to cool.

The pickling liquid can be stored in an airtight container for 1 month in the fridge.

MAKES **4** CUPS
PREP: **10** MINUTES + AT LEAST **72** HOURS PICKLING TIME

Pink Pickled Turnips

Serve as a tangy, colorful accompaniment to sandwiches, grilled meats, and meze platters.

INGREDIENTS
4 cloves garlic
2 large turnips, cut into 2-inch batons
2 small beets, cut into 2-inch batons
2 tsp coriander seeds
2 tsp cumin seeds
1 tsp black pepper
4 cups hot Pickling Liquid (page 173)

In a large sterilized jar, combine all ingredients except pickling liquid. Pour hot pickling liquid over vegetables, ensuring they are fully submerged. Seal the jar tightly. Store in a cool, dry place for at least 72 hours to allow the flavors to develop.

Pickles can be stored in an airtight container for 1 month in the fridge.

PRESERVE NOW *Canadians have a deep-rooted tradition of preserving food, born from harsh winters incapable of providing fresh produce. Buy fruits and vegetables seasonally, and pickle, preserve, ferment, jam, or jellify them for the winter months. When done right, homemade preserves are far better than store-bought alternatives and cost much less. Robert Lemieux's garden in Shawville, Quebec, yields summer produce, from bursting heirloom tomatoes to crisp cucumbers and fiery peppers. By preserving these, his family enjoys vibrant snacks and meals all winter long.*

MAKES **4** CUPS
PREP: **10** MINUTES + AT LEAST **72** HOURS PICKLING TIME

Spicy Dill Pickles

INGREDIENTS
6 cloves garlic
4 long red peppers
2 large cucumbers, quartered into spears
1 fennel, quartered
Bunch of dill
1 Tbsp coriander seeds
1 tsp celery seeds
4 cups hot Pickling Liquid (page 173)

In a large sterilized jar, combine all ingredients except pickling liquid. Pour hot pickling liquid over vegetables, ensuring they are fully submerged. Seal the jar tightly. Store in a cool, dry place for at least 72 hours to allow the flavors to develop.

Pickles can be stored in an airtight container for 1 month in the fridge.

MAKES **2** CUPS
PREP: **15** MINUTES

Muddled Berries

INGREDIENTS
½ cup hulled and chopped strawberries
½ cup blackberries, chopped
½ cup raspberries, chopped
½ cup blueberries
1½ Tbsp sugar
1 tsp lemon zest
2 tsp lemon juice
2 tsp thinly sliced mint
1 tsp thinly sliced lemon verbena
1 tsp thinly sliced lemon balm
¼ tsp pink pepper
Pinch of salt
Pinch of black pepper

In a small bowl, combine berries, sugar, and lemon zest and juice. Set aside for 3 minutes to macerate.

In a stand mixer fitted with a whisk attachment, combine all ingredients and whip on low speed for 4–6 minutes.

Serve cold, either as a topping for desserts, pancakes, or yogurt or as a refreshing standalone treat.

Berries can be stored in an airtight container for 2 days in the fridge.

MAKES **4** CUPS
PREP: **5** MINUTES

Whipped Honey Butter

In this recipe, I use European butter, which has a higher butterfat content and makes for a creamy, rich, and luxurious spread. Look for it at specialty grocery stores, gourmet markets, or online.

INGREDIENTS
3 Tbsp honey
2 Tbsp maple syrup
1 lb European butter, softened
1 Tbsp salt

Combine all ingredients in a stand mixer fitted with a whisk attachment and whisk for 2 minutes, until airy. Serve at room temperature.

Butter can be stored in an airtight container for 2 weeks in the fridge.

MAKES **2** CUPS
PREP: **10** MINUTES + **1** WEEK STANDING TIME / COOK TIME: **5** MINUTES

Chili-Garlic Oil

INGREDIENTS
2 cups canola oil
4 star anise
¼ cup chili flakes
2 Tbsp finely chopped garlic
2 Tbsp finely chopped shallots
2 Tbsp finely chopped scallions
1 Tbsp green peppercorns
1 Tbsp pink peppercorns
1 Tbsp white peppercorns
1 Tbsp Szechuan peppercorns
1 Tbsp chopped long pepper
1 Tbsp black pepper

Pour oil into a deep saucepan and heat to a temperature of 350°F.

Combine the remaining ingredients in a medium sterilized glass jar. Pour in hot oil, then set the mixture aside to cool. Seal the jar and set aside for 1 week at room temperature.

The chili oil can be stored in an airtight container for 30 days in the fridge.

MAKES **2** CUPS
PREP: **10** MINUTES / COOK TIME: **35–55** MINUTES

Cola-Caramelized Onions

INGREDIENTS

1 cup (2 sticks) butter
4–5 white onions, thinly sliced
4 cloves garlic
6 sprigs thyme
2 bay leaves
¼ cup Hennessy
4 tsp brown sugar
1 tsp salt
1 tsp black pepper
1 cup Coca-Cola
1 Tbsp soy sauce

Melt butter in a medium cast-iron skillet over medium heat. Add onions, garlic, thyme, and bay leaves. Sauté for 5-8 minutes, until translucent. Pour in Hennessy and deglaze.

Add brown sugar, salt, and pepper. Pour in cola and soy sauce. Simmer over medium-low heat for 30-45 minutes, until jammy. Set aside to cool.

Onions can be stored in an airtight container for 5 days in the fridge.

MAKES **1** GALLON
PREP: **10** MINUTES / COOK TIME: **~1** HOUR

Stewed Tomatoes and Basil

INGREDIENTS

24 vine-ripened tomatoes
¼ cup olive oil
18 cloves garlic
3 bunches basil, tied with butcher's twine
½ cup + 2 tsp sugar
3 tsp flaky sea salt
3 tsp black pepper
6 cups tomato juice
¾ cup white wine vinegar

Bring a large saucepan of water to a boil. Core tomatoes, then score the bottom with an 'X'. Add tomatoes to the water and boil for 30 seconds. Transfer them to a bowl of ice water and set aside for 1 minute. Remove tomatoes and peel off the skins. Quarter tomatoes.

Heat oil in a Dutch oven over medium-high heat. Add garlic and sauté for 1 minute, until fragrant. Add tomatoes and the remaining ingredients and bring to a boil. Reduce heat to medium-low and simmer for 1 hour, stirring occasionally, until tomatoes are tender. Set aside to cool.

Remove the butcher's twine from basil. Transfer the stewed tomato mixture into sterilized glass jars and seal.

The stewed tomatoes can be stored in airtight containers for 3 months in a cool, dry place.

FARRO THE LOVE OF GRAINS *For a great side dish, sauté ¼ cup of stewed tomatoes with a knob of butter and ¾ cup of precooked farro until heated through.*

MAKES **2** CUPS
PREP: **10** MINUTES / COOK TIME: ~**2** HOURS

Caitlyn's Curry Ketchup

INGREDIENTS
1 Tbsp curry powder
2 tsp paprika
1 tsp garlic powder
1 tsp onion powder
1 Tbsp butter
1 Tbsp finely chopped onions
2 cloves garlic, finely chopped
1 Tbsp white wine
5 sprigs thyme
2 bay leaves
1 cup brown sugar
½ cup tomato paste
½ cup tomato juice
½ cup tomato purée
¼ cup red wine vinegar
1 Tbsp Worcestershire sauce
1 Tbsp molasses
Salt and black pepper, to taste

Combine spices in a small bowl.

Melt butter in a medium cast-iron saucepan over medium-high heat. Add onions and garlic and sauté for 2–3 minutes, until translucent. Add the spice mix and heat for 30 seconds, stirring constantly, until fragrant.

Add wine and simmer for 3–4 minutes, until reduced. Add the remaining ingredients and bring to a boil. Reduce heat to low and simmer for 2 hours. Discard thyme and bay leaves.

While still hot, transfer the mixture to a blender and blend until smooth. Set aside to cool.

The ketchup can be stored in an airtight container for 1 month in the fridge.

INTUITION ON A PLATE *In Malaysian culture, the term **aga aga** embodies an intuitive approach to cooking, where each cook adds "a little bit of this and a little bit of that" based on personal preference. This method lends a unique, distinctive flavor to every dish. It's a subtle, almost secret technique that enhances taste and captivates guests, leaving their palates delightfully enchanted.*

a guide to soup stocks

A well-made stock is the foundation of exceptional soups, sauces, and countless other dishes. This chart outlines the essential elements of various stocks, from the bones or vegetables used to the aromatic additions that elevate their flavors. Whether you're crafting a light vegetable velouté or a robust demi-glace, this guide provides the essential ratios and cooking times for success.

	BONES	MIREPOIX	AROMATICS	WATER	TIME	RESULTS
VEGETABLE	3 LBS	1 LB	MUSHROOMS ALLIUM	11½ CUPS	**60** MINUTES	MUSHROOM VELOUTÉ
POULTRY	3 LBS	1 LB	CORIANDER GINGER ORANGE	11½ CUPS	**4–6** HOURS	CHICKEN PHO
MEAT	3 LBS	1 LB	WINE ROSEMARY BERRY	11½ CUPS	**8–12** HOURS	GASTRIQUE OR DEMI-GLACE
SEAFOOD	3 LBS	1 LB	SAFFRON CITRUS HERBS	11½ CUPS	**45** MINUTES	BISQUE
FISH	3 LBS	1 LB	LEEKS LEMON GARLIC WHITE WINE	11½ CUPS	**45** MINUTES	DASHI
POT LIQUOR	ANY	1 LB	BOURBON APPLES PARSLEY	11½ CUPS	**3** HOURS	SAUCE ROBERT

METRIC CONVERSION CHART

VOLUME

IMPERIAL/U.S.	METRIC
⅛ TSP	0.5 ML
¼ TSP	1 ML
½ TSP	2.5 ML
¾ TSP	4 ML
1 TSP	5 ML
½ TBSP	8 ML
1 TBSP	15 ML
1½ TBSP	23 ML
2 TBSP	30 ML
¼ CUP	60 ML
⅓ CUP	80 ML
½ CUP	125 ML
⅔ CUP	165 ML
¾ CUP	185 ML
1 CUP	250 ML
1¼ CUPS	310 ML
1⅓ CUPS	330 ML
1½ CUPS	375 ML
1⅔ CUPS	415 ML
1¾ CUPS	435 ML
2 CUPS	500 ML
2¼ CUPS	560 ML
2⅓ CUPS	580 ML
2½ CUPS	625 ML
2¾ CUPS	690 ML
3 CUPS	750 ML
4 CUPS / 1 QUART	1 L
5 CUPS	1.25 L
6 CUPS	1.5 L
7 CUPS	1.75 L
8 CUPS	2 L
12 CUPS	3 L
16 CUPS	4 L

LIQUID MEASURES (ALCOHOL)

IMPERIAL/U.S.	METRIC
½ FL OZ	15 ML
1 FL OZ	30 ML
2 FL OZ	60 ML
3 FL OZ	90 ML
4 FL OZ	120 ML

CANS AND JARS

IMPERIAL/U.S.	METRIC
6 OZ	170 ML
10 OZ	300 ML
14 OZ	398 ML
19 OZ	540 ML
28 OZ	796 ML

WEIGHT

IMPERIAL/U.S.	METRIC
½ OZ	15 G
1 OZ	30 G
2 OZ	60 G
3 OZ	85 G
4 OZ (¼ LB)	115 G
5 OZ	140 G
6 OZ	170 G
7 OZ	200 G
8 OZ (½ LB)	225 G
9 OZ	255 G
10 OZ	285 G
11 OZ	310 G
12 OZ (¾ LB)	340 G
13 OZ	370 G
14 OZ	400 G
15 OZ	425 G
16 OZ (1 LB)	450 G
1¼ LBS	570 G
1½ LBS	675 G
2 LBS	900 G
3 LBS	1.4 KG
4 LBS	1.8 KG
5 LBS	2.3 KG
6 LBS	2.7 KG

LINEAR

IMPERIAL/U.S.	METRIC
⅛ INCH	3 MM
¼ INCH	6 MM
½ INCH	12 MM
¾ INCH	2 CM
1 INCH	2.5 CM
1¼ INCHES	3 CM
1½ INCHES	3.5 CM
1¾ INCHES	4.5 CM
2 INCHES	5 CM
2½ INCHES	6.5 CM
3 INCHES	7.5 CM
4 INCHES	10 CM
5 INCHES	12.5 CM
6 INCHES	15 CM
7 INCHES	18 CM
10 INCHES	25 CM
12 INCHES (1 FOOT)	30 CM
13 INCHES	33 CM
16 INCHES	41 CM
18 INCHES	46 CM
24 INCHES (2 FEET)	60 CM
28 INCHES	70 CM
30 INCHES	75 CM
6 FEET	1.8 M

NON-OVEN TEMPERATURE

IMPERIAL/U.S.	METRIC
81°F	27°C
90°F	32°C
120°F	49°C
125°F	52°C
130°F	54°C
140°F	60°C
150°F	66°C
155°F	68°C
160°F	71°C
165°F	74°C
167°F	75°C
170°F	77°C
175°F	80°C
180°F	82°C
190°F	88°C
200°F	93°C
240°F	116°C
250°F	121°C
300°F	149°C
325°F	163°C
350°F	177°C
360°F	182°C
375°F	191°C

OVEN TEMPERATURE

IMPERIAL/U.S.	METRIC
200°F	95°C
250°F	120°C
275°F	135°C
300°F	150°C
325°F	160°C
350°F	180°C
375°F	190°C
400°F	200°C
425°F	220°C
450°F	230°C
500°F	260°C
550°F	290°C

BAKING PANS

IMPERIAL/U.S.	METRIC
5 x 9-INCH LOAF PAN	2 L LOAF PAN
9 x 13-INCH CAKE PAN	4 L CAKE PAN
11 x 17-INCH BAKING SHEET	30 x 45-CM BAKING SHEET

ACKNOWLEDGMENTS

First and foremost, thank you to the Land of the Algonquin.

Countless people and organizations have made a significant impact on my career, including my culinary mentor Chef Almir Da Fonseca, my service and wine mentor Sean Fry, and the educators at the Culinary Institute of America.

Thank you to the chefs who graciously took me under their wing: Chef Matthew Kirkley (COI), Chef Raj Dixit (Michael Mina), Shifu Robin Lim (Eight Tables), Chef Mikey Adams (Villon), and the team behind Fäviken. And to Rahil Rathod for coaching me and pushing me farther.

I'd like to extend my gratitude to my mentor Robert Lemieux, who always pushed me to respect the integrity of the table.

Above all, the entire team at Aiāna—past and present—thank you for everything you do as none of this would be possible without you. This includes Catherine, Chiron, Connor, Jack, Jordan, Josh, Juju, Justin, Marita, Oliwier, Pranav, Reta, Sean, and Sergei.

Thank you to Alan. Thank you for your endless kindness and for being the ultimate teammate. I can't wait to share recipes, flavors, and plenty of laughs in the kitchen with you!

INDEX

Page numbers in italics refer to photos.

c

d

m

n

ABOUT THE AUTHOR

Chef Raghav Chaudhary, owner of the acclaimed Aiāna in Ottawa, celebrates Canada's multicultural heritage through seasonally inspired dishes. Under his leadership, Aiāna has earned multiple accolades, including Best New Restaurant and a nomination for Restaurant of the Year at the Ottawa Culinary Awards, as well as recognition in Canada's Top 100 Restaurants. In 2024, he proudly represented Ottawa at the Canadian Culinary Championship. He supports community causes such as the Ottawa Mission and the Shepherds of Good Hope.

Trained in prestigious kitchens worldwide, Raghav masterfully blends seasonal flavors with modern techniques. Dedicated to sustainability and locally sourced ingredients, he continues to inspire with his innovative cuisine and community contributions. He resides in Ottawa.

@dineaiana
aiana.ca

AITANA

With curiosity at its heart, *Gather, Savor, Share* is a beautiful testament to the power food has to connect us. From a quick Monday-night stir fry to a lavish weekend feast, each and every meal does more than fill our bellies – it nourishes our spirit and inspires our collective sense of belonging.